STUDIO PRESS

First published in the UK in 2024 by Studio Press,
an imprint of Bonnier Books UK,
4th Floor, Victoria House, Bloomsbury Square, London WC1B 4DA
Owned by Bonnier Books,
Sveavägen 56, Stockholm, Sweden
bonnierbooks.co.uk

1 3 5 7 9 10 8 6 4 2

ISBN 978-1-80078-940-1

MIX
Paper | Supporting
responsible forestry
FSC
www.fsc.org **FSC® C104723**

A CIP catalogue record for this book is available from the British Library

Disney

Tim Burton's THE NIGHTMARE BEFORE CHRISTMAS

THE FULL FILM SCRIPT

By Bill Scollon and Barbara Montini

S
STUDIO
PRESS

INTRODUCTION

"*The Nightmare Before Christmas* is deeper in my heart than any other film. It is more beautiful than I imagined it would be. I know I will never have this feeling again," Tim Burton said upon the completion of his film in 1993.

These humble and heartfelt words from Burton are not surprising since this film—this funny, poignant, quirky, and, yes, a touch scary, film—in many ways, *is* Tim Burton.

The first iteration of *Tim Burton's The Nightmare Before Christmas* was a poem, a take on Clement Clarke Moore's "A Visit from St. Nicholas" (commonly known as "The Night Before Christmas"). Burton wrote the poem in the early 1980s while working as a somewhat discontented animator at The Walt Disney Company. He didn't quite fit the mold of the internationally perceived Disney image and was disinterested in working on stories about cute, animated, anthropomorphic animals. "I just couldn't do it," Burton recalled. "I couldn't even fake the Disney style."

Nevertheless, Burton's supervisors recognized his innate talent, and the studio allotted him budgets to produce two original short films. The first was *Vincent*, a well-received stop-motion animated story of a boy who imagines himself to be the legendary horror film actor Vincent Price (who, to Burton's delight, agreed to narrate the film). The second production was *Frankenweenie*, a live-action film about a boy who brings his dog back to life. *Frankenweenie* was slated to open the bill in theaters presenting the 1984 re-release of *Pinocchio*. Unfortunately, when Burton's film was given a PG rating, the plans for its release were shelved.

Burton's first sketches for a film based on his poem "The Nightmare Before Christmas" were done while he was making *Vincent*. The original poem had just three characters: the spindly protagonist Jack Skellington, his dog Zero, and Santa Claus. "Nightmare" is not a typical Christmas story. It's not even a typical Halloween story. But it is exactly a Tim Burton story, one that explores themes of loneliness, searching for self, and wanting something more out of life but being unsure of how to find it. It's also rich with motifs about kindness, love, and, ultimately, about being comfortable in your own skin. It's about understanding that being different is not just okay, it's wonderful. The fact that "Nightmare" is filled with such human themes, housed in an unexpected setting with unusual characters, makes perfect sense when you consider the man who created it. The story is an amalgamation of Burton's own emotions, curiosities, and interests that he'd had throughout his life.

Timothy Walter Burton ~~was born~~ on August 28, 1958. He grew up in the Los Angeles suburb of Burbank, California, but felt out of step with what he saw as the blandness of suburban life. Burbank in the 1960s was a factory town with Lockheed Aircraft, the aeronautical manufacturing powerhouse, at one end of town and moviemakers The Walt Disney Studios and Warner Bros. at the other. Burton was a shy, introverted child who spent his time "seeing horror movies, watching television, and playing in the local cemetery," he recalled. But Burton never thought of cemeteries as creepy or uncomfortable and instead likens them to museums. In his mind, the two places share similar qualities. "Both have a quiet, introspective, yet electrifying atmosphere," Burton explained. "Excitement, mystery, discovery, life, and death all in one place."

Burton began drawing at a young age. With his restless imagination and feelings of alienation, drawing became both an emotional and creative outlet for the quiet kid with the humorous and high-spirited point of view. "If I'm doing a drawing, I can become focused," he said. "It's a calming experience, and that's something I've never forgotten."

Many of Burton's early sketches are filled with fantastic—and sometimes frightful—images prompted by his imagination and the movies and television shows he liked to watch. He was absorbed by films such as *Jason and the Argonauts*, with its classic stop-action sequences. He loved old monster movies and was never afraid, believing that "most monsters are misperceived."

On the other side of the coin, Dr. Seuss was Burton's favorite children's author. Burton loved the books for their playful rhymes and whimsical art. One of his greatest hopes for "Nightmare" was to make it into a TV holiday special that would become a seasonal favorite, like Dr. Seuss' *How the Grinch Stole Christmas!*, a wonderfully off-beat parable narrated by Boris Karloff, the actor most famous for playing Frankenstein's monster.

Along with drawing, Burton made homemade movies with his friends, including a jerky stop-motion animated film using action toys. "It was really bad and it shows how little [I knew] about animation at the beginning," Burton said.

For his live-action films, Burton created characters for himself to portray like Doctor of Doom and Rigger T. Mortis, celebrated evil geniuses who lived exciting lives filled with daring and adventure. But still, feeling lonely, being at loose ends, and yearning for something more were themes that Burton understood well and would later become driving forces for the story of Jack Skellington, Burton's own misperceived monster.

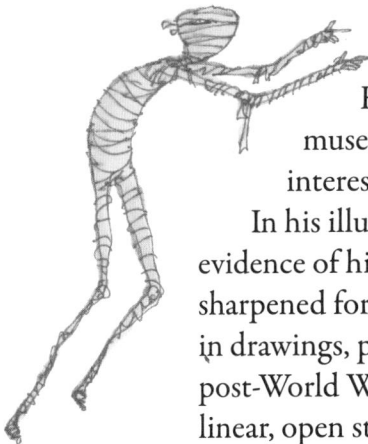

———————

Burton joked once that unless you counted the Hollywood Wax Museum, he had never visited a museum until he was a teenager. But as he matured, his interests and influences grew.

In his illustrations, drawn when he was in his early twenties, the evidence of his expanding horizons is present: the twisted structures, sharpened forms, and distortions of German Expressionism found in drawings, paintings, and films like *The Cabinet of Dr. Caligari*; the post-World War II mid-century modern designs with their clean, linear, open style filled with color; the Bauhaus School, where art is coupled with function; and the pen-and-ink drawings of artists such as Edward Gorey and Ronald Searle, with their intricate textures and crosshatching. These influences, combined with Burton's appreciation of pop culture and commercial art, make *Nightmare* a visual feast that could only come from the mind of Tim Burton.

But while *Nightmare* was conceived, shaped, and championed by Burton, it took a team of talented collaborators to execute his vision on-screen. Although Burton himself was not on the set, the highly gifted team respected his concept, and in turn Burton trusted them completely to bring his story to life. The fact that such an out-of-the-box thinker could create something so personal and beautiful and then entrust it to others to bring it to life is remarkable.

The film is simply a masterpiece whose hold on the public imagination has strengthened and grown in the decades since its release. And, perhaps most wonderful of all, *Tim Burton's The Nightmare Before Christmas* has secured its place as one of the greatest holiday films of all time, a fact that Burton acknowledges with a simple, "I know. Crazy. It's weird."

———

Inside this book you'll find the complete film transcription for *Tim Burton's The Nightmare Before Christmas*, along with the lyrics for each song. The book includes a collection of behind-the-scenes stories and insights from the animators, producers, writers, artists, and technicians who came together to produce this groundbreaking film. A wealth of curated animation art, graphics, and photographs from Disney's storied Animation Research Library, Walt Disney Archives, and personal collections bring the making-of story uniquely to life. As Jack Skellington would say, "Isn't that wonderful? It couldn't be more wonderful!"

Tim Burton once reflected that, as a kid, "Those crude stop-motion animation holiday things that were on year in [and] year out made an impact on you early and stayed with you. I had grown up with those and had a real feeling for them, and I think, without being too direct, the impulse was to do something like that."

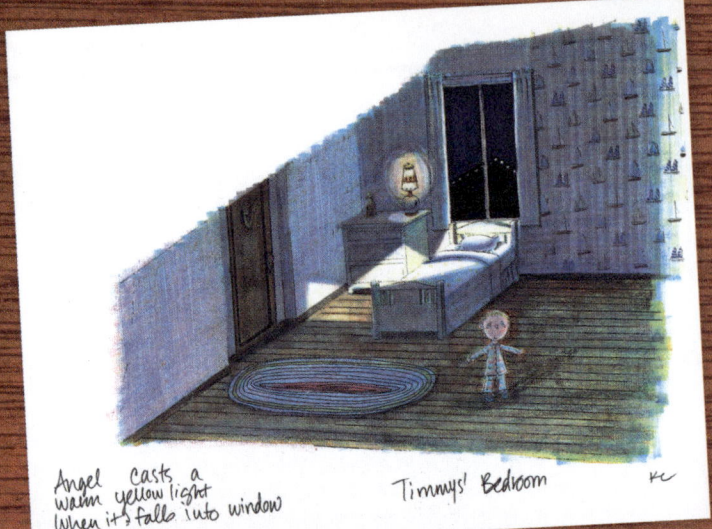

Angel casts a
warm yellow light
when it falls into window

Timmys! Bedroom   KC

EGGSALAD SANDWICH

SEQ. 800/SHOT #3

SIZE / POSITION OF
MOON T.B.D. PROJECTED
"OOGIE BOOGIE" AS 13th
GIFT.

8° DIA.

FRONT ELEVATION GIFT BOXES IN "OPEN" POSITION.

DISNEY THEME PARKS' HAUNTED MANSIONS receive a *Tim Burton's The Nightmare Before Christmas* makeover nearly every Halloween. This stack of gift boxes, with pop-up characters and creatures, greets guests as they step into their ride vehicles. The design came from Disney's Entertainment Partners with designer Richard Improta creating the pencil drawing and Tim Wollweber designing the characters, the boxes, and their movements. A projection of Oogie Boogie appears above it all, the position of which, as of this rendering, was still to be determined.

DISNEY
TIM BURTON'S
THE NIGHTMARE BEFORE CHRISTMAS

Story
by
Tim Burton
Michael McDowell
Caroline Thompson

Lyrics
by
Danny Elfman

Screenplay
by
Caroline Thompson

SEQ · 1400/2

TIM BURTON'S THE NIGHTMARE BEFORE CHRISTMAS emerged from
Michael Eisner's 1984 pledge to bring a new era of ideas and products to The Walt
Disney Company, which was facing the prospect of being broken up and sold
off to outside investors. At the time of its completion, Disney executive Jeffrey
Katzenberg stated, "In the eight years I've been at the studio, the only other movie
that really set out to do something unlike anything done before was *Who Framed
Roger Rabbit*. I consider this to be a sister film."

EXT. WILDERNESS - DAWN

Camera moves down toward a circular grove of trees. Each
of the trees have a door, which is painted in the form of
holiday symbols, on their trunks.

                    SANTA CLAUS (OFF)
          'Twas a long time ago
          Longer now than it seems
          In a place that perhaps
          You've seen in your dreams

Camera tilts up to reveal two trees, which have an Easter
egg shaped door and a Thanksgiving turkey shaped door on
their trunks.

                    SANTA CLAUS (CONT'D)

          For the story that you
          Are about to be told
          Took place in the holiday
          Worlds of old
          Now, you've probably wondered
          Where holidays come from

Camera dollies off the trees with the turkey and Easter
egg and past a tree with a Christmas tree painted on it, to
reveal a tree, which has a Halloween pumpkin painted on it.

                    SANTA CLAUS (CONT'D)

          If you haven't I'd say
          It's time you begun . . .

The Halloween pumpkin door on the tree swings open. Camera
dollies in to the darkness inside the tree.

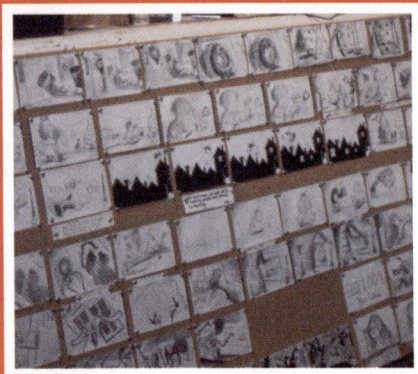

KATZENBERG MEETING

After establishing himself as an A-list film director, Tim Burton returned to Disney to see about resurrecting his pet project. *Tim Burton's The Nightmare Before Christmas* illustrations, notes, and poem had been languishing in the Disney archives for ten years, but now the wheels were in motion to develop the project. Everything hinged on the outcome of one final meeting with the chairman of The Walt Disney Studios, Jeffrey Katzenberg.

To prepare for the meeting, Burton assembled his team to demonstrate the concept's viability. Burton's producing partner Denise Di Novi was on board, and a twenty-second test film was made by stop-motion animators under the direction of Henry Selick, considered by many to be the best in the business. Composer Danny Elfman put together music samples, and Burton's longtime creative collaborator, Rick Heinrichs, who had made the original Jack puppet ten years before, pulled together additional sample puppets and props.

It was late in the day and Katzenberg was running behind schedule. Finally, as Heinrichs tells it, the energetic executive came into the room, asking, "All right, what have you got here?" Heinrichs and the others presented the test film, the puppets, props, and set pieces. Lastly, Burton pressed the play button on a portable cassette player, and Elfman's song samples filled the room. "He lit up," Heinrichs said. After all the years of hoping to get *Nightmare* made, it was exciting and gratifying to finally get the green light. "Go, do it," Katzenberg said. Heinrichs grinned and thought to himself, "Oh, so this is how Hollywood works."

PULLING IDEAS FROM VARIOUS PEOPLE and sources to create the best scenes possible was part of the culture of the *Nightmare* production team. When Jack does his scarecrow dance in an early scene, Animator Paul Berry not only revisited the scarecrow scenes in the 1939 classic *The Wizard of Oz*, but Director Henry Selick (above) also performed his conception of the dance. Even a production assistant with dance training, Beth Schneider, contributed her ideas for how to bring the scarecrow dance to life.

INT. HALLOWEEN TREE - NIGHT

Camera moves in through the darkness to reveal a huge jack-o'-lantern scarecrow. A sign on the jack-o'-lantern scarecrow reads Halloween Town. Camera moves in, off the scarecrow.

Camera moves in through the darkness, then a door on the other side of the tree opens to reveal the Halloween Town cemetery. The cemetery is composed of a series of decrepit tombstones, with ghostly shadows of a shadow chorus on them.

Tim Burton had always imagined that Tim Burton's The Nightmare Before Christmas *would be a musical "in the same way those holiday specials always had music,"* he recalled. *With only his notes and sketches in hand, Burton called upon his friend and frequent collaborator, composer Danny Elfman, to write the songs he felt would be integral to the story. Elfman recalled there was some sense of urgency since the film's director, Henry Selick, had been hiring crew, leasing equipment, and buying supplies and was "ready to start shooting,"* Elfman said. *"And Tim said, 'Let's start doing songs.' He would bring his drawings and lay them out on the table. It was a very organic way of developing a musical."*

THIS IS HALLOWEEN

Boys and girls of every age
Wouldn't you like to see something strange?
Come with us and you will see
This our town of Halloween
This is Halloween, this is Halloween
Pumpkins scream in the dead of night

This is Halloween everybody make a scene
Trick or treat till the neighbor's gonna die of fright
It's our town. Everybody scream
In this town of Halloween

I am the one hiding under your bed
Teeth ground sharp and eyes glowing red
I am the one hiding under your stairs
Fingers like snakes and spiders in my hair

This is Halloween, this is Halloween,
Halloween, Halloween,
Halloween, Halloween.

In this town we call home
Everyone hail to the pumpkin song
In this town, don't we love it now
Everybody's waiting for the next surprise

Round that corner, man, hiding in the trash cans
Something's waiting now to pounce and how you'll scream

This is Halloween
Red and black and slimy green
Aren't you scared?
Well, that's just fine

Say it once, say it twice,
Take a chance and roll the dice
Ride with the moon in the dead of night
Everybody scream, everybody scream
In our town of Halloween

I am the clown with the tear-away face
Here in a flash and gone without a trace
I am the who when you call who's there
I am the wind blowing through your hair
I am the shadow on the moon at night
Filling your dreams to the brim with fright

This is Halloween, this is Halloween
Halloween, Halloween
Halloween, Halloween

Tender Lumplings everywhere
Life's no fun without a good scare
That's our job
But we're not mean
In our town of Halloween

In this town don't we love it now
Everyone's waiting for the next surprise

Skeleton Jack might catch you in the back
And scream like a banshee
Make you jump out of your skin
This is Halloween, everybody scream

Would you please make way for a very special guy
Our man Jack is king of the pumpkin patch
Everyone hail to the Pumpkin King now
This is Halloween, this is Halloween
Halloween, Halloween
Halloween, Halloween

In this town we call home
Everyone hail to the pumpkin song

La-la-la-la, la-la-la-la, Halloween, Halloween
La-la-la-la, la-la-la-la, Halloween, Halloween
La-la-la-la, la-la-la-la, Halloween, Halloween
La, la, la, la —Woo!

While many of the characters in the film were created by Tim Burton, his unique and defining style also influenced the artists as they designed and created additional characters. Art Director Deane Taylor and his artists created the many additional characters needed to flesh out the story, all in a very Burtonesque style and all subject to his approval.

ANOTHER NIGHT
BEFORE CHRISTMAS

Tim Burton's inspiration for *Tim Burton's The Nightmare Before Christmas* came from the poem "A Visit from St. Nicholas," known more commonly as "The Night Before Christmas." The poem first appeared on December 23, 1823, in *The Sentinel*, the local paper for Troy, New York. The author was unnamed at the time, but years later, Clement Clarke Moore took credit for the work, though there are those who believe it was actually written by a New York writer named Henry Livingston Jr.

The poem gave audiences a new spin on the character of St. Nicholas, also known as Santa Claus, who had traditionally been depicted as a somewhat stern man with a thinner build who traveled by horse. This older description was derived from a combination of several legends, including the British Father Christmas, the Dutch Sinterklaas, and a fourth-century bishop, St. Nicholas of Myra. The Santa of "A Visit From St. Nicholas" was a jolly, plump elf with a red nose, rosy cheeks, dimples, and a twinkle in his eye. Instead of a horse, he traveled in a sleigh pulled by flying reindeer, all of whom had fanciful names such as Dancer, Prancer, and Cupid. This reinvented vision of Santa proved immensely popular and became the model for the Christmas icon known today.

This cultural image of Santa was the perfect foil for the mind of Tim Burton. As a child, it seemed to him that his two favorite holidays, Halloween and Christmas, just naturally bumped into each other. Burton loved watching the annual airings of the TV specials *How the Grinch Stole Christmas!* and *Rudolph the Red-Nosed Reindeer*, two animated classics that further stirred Burton's creative juices for a holiday mash-up.

Using Moore's classic composition as a jumping off point, Burton wrote his poem, "The Nightmare Before Christmas," while working at Disney. His initial thought was that the poem would make a good children's book, so he had done numerous drawings of the poem's three characters, Jack, Zero, and Santa Claus. Shortly after, Burton created a story outline that was expanded while working on the songs with Danny Elfman. More characters were added along the way, including Jack's nemesis, Oogie Boogie, who was inspired by Burton's memory of a character from Betty Boop cartoons voiced by the popular big band leader Cab Calloway.

Tim Burton's The Nightmare Before Christmas not only broke the mold of Moore's original telling of Christmas Eve, but for many it has also become an enduring part of the season, transcending from a cult classic to a genuine holiday classic. When the film was first released under the Touchstone Pictures banner, it was hailed as a triumph by The Walt Disney Company. "I think the film's breathtaking," said Jeffrey Katzenberg, then chairman of The Walt Disney Studios. "There is nothing more rewarding for a studio to be able to do than surprise and captivate movie audiences. *The Nightmare Before Christmas* is a visual treat. It has great heart and soul."

EXT. HALLOWEEN TOWN - NIGHT

Camera dollies across the creatures as they wave their hands at Jack. Creatures start to bow toward Jack. Sally, standing in front of the Hanging Tree, applauds at Jack.

Jack stands atop the fountain as the creatures, circled around him, applaud. Camera dollies back and cranes up into a high angle.

The two witches, sitting on a stone wall, look at one another and laugh uproariously.

Big Witch and Small Witch laugh. They take off their hats and throw them into the air. The Clown and the Behemoth look at one another and smile.

                    CLOWN
        It's over!

                    BEHEMOTH
        We did it.

The Clown and the Behemoth bump their stomachs against one another. The Wolfman leans toward two other inhabitants of Halloween Town, Mr. Hyde and Cyclops.

                    WOLFMAN
        Wasn't it terrifying?

                MR. HYDE & CYCLOPS
                    (in unison)
        What a night!

Jack stands on the fountain as the Mayor gestures at the creatures.

                    MAYOR
                (optimistic face)
        Great Halloween, everybody.

Jack steps beside the Mayor, then he gestures at the creatures.

> JACK
>
> I believe it was our most horrible yet. Thank you,
everyone.

The Mayor gestures at Jack.

> MAYOR
> (optimistic face)
> No. Thanks to you, Jack.

A vampire and the Mayor look up at Jack.

> MAYOR (CONT'D)
> (optimistic face)
> Without your brilliant leadership . . .

> JACK
> (overlapping)
> Not at all, Mayor.

The vampire, standing amidst the creatures, gestures at Jack.

> VAMPIRE
> You're such a scream, Jack.

Big Witch enters and walks toward Jack.

> BIG WITCH
> You're a witch's fondest dream.

Small Witch enters, then she stops and looks up at Jack with
admiration.

> SMALL WITCH
> You made walls fall, Jack.

Sally gazes adoringly at Jack.

> BIG WITCH
> Walls fall? You made the very mountains crack, Jack.

Dr. Finkelstein's hand enters and grabs Sally. Dr. Finkelstein, a ghoulish creature who sits in a wheelchair, jerks Sally toward him.

                    DR. FINKELSTEIN
          The deadly nightshade you slipped me wore off, Sally.

Sally tries to jerk away from Dr. Finkelstein's grasp.

                    SALLY
                   (groans)
          Let go.

                    DR. FINKELSTEIN
          You're not ready for so much excitement.

                    SALLY
                   (groans)
          Yes, I am.

Dr. Finkelstein turns his wheelchair and tries to drag Sally behind him.

                    DR. FINKELSTEIN
          You're coming with me.

                    SALLY
                   (groans)
          No, I'm not.

Sally pulls apart some stitches in her arm. Sally falls as Dr. Finkelstein, sitting in his wheelchair, pulls her arm off her body.

Sally yelps.

Sally exits as Dr. Finkelstein falls to the ground. Dr. Finkelstein waves Sally's arm at Sally.

                    DR. FINKELSTEIN
          Come back here, you foolish . . .

Sally's arm starts to hit Dr. Finkelstein in the head.

DR. FINKELSTEIN (CONT'D)
Ow. Ow. Ow-w-w.

Camera moves past an Undersea Gal to Jack, who smiles at her. The
Undersea Gal, a reptilian creature with claws, looks at Jack.

UNDERSEA GAL
Oh Jack, you made wounds ooze and flesh crawl.

Jack walks backwards as the creatures enter and move toward
him. Jack waves his hands dismissingly at the creatures.

JACK
Thank you. Thank you. Thank you. Very much.

MAYOR
(optimistic face, over speaker)
Hold it.

The creatures turn and look at the Mayor.

MAYOR (CONT'D)
(optimistic face, over speaker)
We haven't given out the prizes yet.

The crowd gasps.

Jack, realizing the crowd has turned their backs to him, smiles,
then he hurries and exits. The Mayor, standing atop his hearse,
holds up a trophy cup.

MAYOR (CONT'D)
(optimistic Face, into microphone)
Our first award goes to the vampires for most blood
drained
in a single evening.

The vampires enter, then they fly and take the trophy cup. Jack
hides behind a corner on a back street of the town.

MAYOR (CONT'D)
(optimistic face, over speaker)
A second and honorable mention goes to the fabulous Dark
Lagoon Leeches.

Jack wipes his brow with relief and sighs.

Jack walks thoughtfully past a skeleton band, three
down-on-their-luck skeletons (a saxophone player, a bass player,
and an accordion player), who are playing a dirge. Jack tosses
a coin into the hat the musicians have placed on the sidewalk.
The saxophone player glances at Jack.

                    SAXOPHONE PLAYER
          Nice work, Bone Daddy.

Jack walks, camera dollying with him as he glances glumly over
his shoulder at the skeleton band.

                    JACK
          Yeah, I guess so. Just like last year.

Past the skeleton band to Jack, who walks glumly
through a gate and out of the town.

                    JACK (CONT'D)
          And the year before that. And the year before that.

EXT. HALLOWEEN LAND - NIGHT

Camera dollies in toward the front gate of the cemetery.

EXT. HALLOWEEN TOWN CEMETERY - NIGHT

Camera dollies in slightly toward Sally, who sits sadly in front
of a tombstone. The sound of Jack's approaching footsteps is
heard.

Sally gasps.

Sally scurries behind a tombstone, then she peers out over the
top of the tombstone. Jack enters through the front gate, then
he closes the gate behind him. Jack walks thoughtfully across
the graveyard, camera dollying with him. Sally, hiding behind
the tombstone, peers at Jack. The tombstone reads: RIP.

Jack's shadow crosses the tombstone, then Sally ducks quickly behind the tombstone. Sally leans around the tombstone, and peers at Jack. Jack walks across the graveyard. Jack walks past a tiny tombstone, which is formed in the shape of a doghouse. The tombstone, which has a carving of a dog on it, reads: Zero. Jack stops, then he slaps his leg. Jack walks and exits. Zero, Jack's ghost dog, materializes from the tombstone. Jack leans thoughtfully against a tombstone. Camera dollies back slightly as Jack sings plaintively.

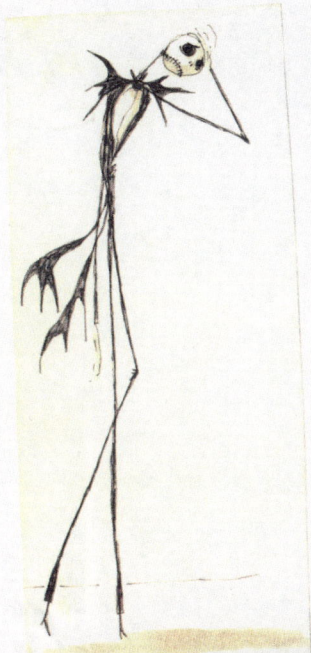

FOR VETERAN ANIMATOR PAUL BERRY, working on *Tim Burton's The Nightmare Before Christmas* was a unique experience. "A lot of time was spent on getting each shot to look great, not only compositionally but also on the level of acting," Berry said. "The amount of energy poured into each shot was unusual. I've never worked on anything like it before." Achieving a high level of acting in a puppet relies on the animator's ability to imbue the inanimate object with realistic human qualities like a slight tilt of the head, the raising of an eyebrow, or a well-timed blink. These types of actions can be very subtle, but when taken together, they breathe life into a performance and create empathy in the viewer.

JACK'S LAMENT

There are few who'd deny at what I do I am the best
For my talents are renowned far and wide
When it comes to surprises in the moonlit night
I excel without ever even trying
With the slightest little effort of my ghostlike charms
I have seen grown men give out a shriek
With a wave of my hand and a well-placed moan
I have swept the very bravest off their feet.

Yet year after year, it's the same routine
And I grow so weary of the sound of screams
And I, Jack, the Pumpkin King
Have grown so tired of the same old thing

Oh, somewhere deep inside of these bones
An emptiness began to grow
There's something out there far from my home
A longing that I've never known

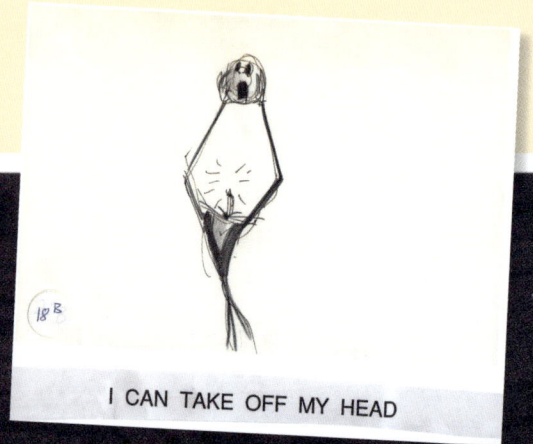

I CAN TAKE OFF MY HEAD

AND I'LL SCARE YOU RIGHT OUT OF YOUR PANTS,

Tim Burton has said it's harder to convey emotion in stop-action animation than it is in cel animation because, in cel animation, there are few limits. If it can be drawn, it can be done. "Three-dimensional animation has limitations because you're moving puppets around," Burton said. "But I think, when it works, it is more effective because it is three-dimensional, and it feels like it's there."

I'm the master of fright, and a demon of light
And I'll scare you right out of your pants
To a guy in Kentucky I'm Mister Unlucky
And I'm known throughout England and France

And since I am dead I can take off my head
To recite Shakespearean quotations
No animal nor man can scream like I can
With the fury of my recitations

But who here would ever understand
That the Pumpkin King with the skeleton grin
Would tire of his crown
If they only understood,
he'd give it all up if he only could.

Oh, there's an empty place in my bones
That calls out for something unknown
The fame and praise come year after year
Does nothing for these empty tears

Jack starts to exit into the wilderness. Sally steps out from behind the tombstone, then she looks up at the off-screen cliff. Sally turns, then she looks down sadly and holds her hands across her heart.

                    SALLY
          Jack, I know how you feel.

Sally walks and exits. Sally staggers between the tombstones, then she drops down to her knees. Sally, kneeling, looks at three tombstones, which have various herbs growing in front of them. The signs on the tombstones read: henbane, witch hazel, deadly nightshade. Sally starts to pick some of the deadly nightshade plants.

INT. DR. FINKELSTEIN'S HOME/KITCHEN - NIGHT

Sally drops the nightshade plants into a jar, which sits on a shelf. The lettering on the jar reads: Deadly Nightshade. Sally puts the jar on a shelf. Dr. Finkelstein's shadow crosses on the wall above a staircase. Sally turns and stares at the shadow.

                    DR. FINKELSTEIN
          Sally!

Dr. Finkelstein enters as he rolls down the staircase on his wheelchair.

                    DR. FINKELSTEIN (CONT'D)
          You've come back.

Sally stares at Dr. Finkelstein.

                    SALLY
          I had to.

                    DR. FINKELSTEIN
          For this.

Dr. Finkelstein's arm enters as he holds up Sally's arm.

                    SALLY
          Yes.

Camera moves past Sally to Dr. Finkelstein, who sits in his
wheelchair and stares at her.

                    DR. FINKELSTEIN
          Shall we, then?

Sally walks up the staircase. Dr. Finkelstein then follows her up
the staircase.

INT. DR. FINKELSTEIN'S HOUSE/LABORATORY - NIGHT

Camera dollies past some test tubes and tables in the laboratory.

                    DR. FINKELSTEIN
          That's twice this month you've slipped deadly . . .

Camera continues to dolly to reveal Sally, strapped to an
operating table, and Dr. Finkelstein, who sits beside her in his
wheelchair. Dr. Finkelstein has sewn Sally's arm back onto her
body.

                    DR. FINKELSTEIN (CONT'D)
          . . . nightshade into my tea and run off.

Sally, strapped to the operating table, smirks at Dr. Finkelstein,
who sits in the wheelchair.

                    SALLY
          Three times.

Dr. Finkelstein leans menacingly toward Sally.

                    DR. FINKELSTEIN
          You're mine, you know. I made you with my own two hands.

Sally gestures at Dr. Finkelstein.

                    SALLY
          You can make other creations. I'm restless. I can't help it.

                    DR. FINKELSTEIN
          It's a phase, my dear. It'll pass.

Dr. Finkelstein bites down on a thread as he finishes sewing on
Sally's arm. Sally looks at him.

FRAME, BY FRAME, BY FRAME . . .

With one camera, one scene, and one animator on an often-cramped stage, the precision process of stop-motion animation can be slow going. An untrained observer could watch an animator work for hours and hours and see very little progress in character movement. Twenty-four single frames—essentially a series of twenty-four still photographs—are needed to produce just one second of stop-motion animation, and, with each frame, the puppet character is moved only slightly to ensure a smooth flow of action. It is painstaking and detailed work that demands extraordinary patience and commitment, but for stop-motion animators, the results are worth the effort.

Animators must also be clever and original. They can be thought of as jacks-of-all-trades because at any point in the day they may need to fix a puppet, touch up some paint, or calculate complicated movements. But above all, they must be excellent actors. They must know each character's style, attitude, and walk, as well as the way they hold themselves and any habitual movements they have, especially because the same animator usually does not work with the same puppet throughout the entire production. And, since consistency is key to the character's believability, every puppet has to appear as if it has been manipulated by the same hands.

"Every character has its own unique repertoire that each animator has to be able to duplicate," Supervising Animator Eric Leighton explained. "Not only must [the animators] all perform it, they must make it believable that it's the same character throughout." Final storyboards and notes from the director gave the animators a road map, but they were always free to improvise action so long as it was true to the character.

The first half of the two-and-a-half-minute scene of Jack singing "Jack's Obsession" was animated by Angie Glocka, but the second half was done by Mike Belzer. But the viewer would never know two different animators worked on the scene because their performances match so perfectly.

Animators also must have a knack for breaking each movement down into seconds and frames, which can be difficult to learn. "It's something that has to be acquired," Glocka said. "Something happens where you start looking at time in a different way. You automatically start breaking action down in a slower time frame. It's like acting but in slow motion. You get into the rhythm and are kind of performing it but very slowly. Concentration is really important."

In the last phase of *Nightmare*'s production, there were nineteen sound stages and fourteen animators working simultaneously, producing about seventy seconds of finished film a week. The average shot in the film lasted about five and a half to six seconds, but there were times when the team did shots lasting ten, fifteen, even twenty seconds, and taking ten days or more to complete. This process could be nerve-wracking, since the smallest error could require a complete reshoot.

Those long camera shots were needed because Director Henry Selick wanted *Nightmare* to have the feel of a live-action musical, with elegant, long, sweeping camera motion. In live-action, the camera would be placed on a dolly or crane to achieve that kind of flow, but manually shooting a fluid movement in one twenty-fourth-of-a-second increments would be impossible. Enter the computer, or in this case the motion control ("mocon") camera.

With the mocon camera, the length, direction, and speed of the camera's movement is programmed into a computer, and the camera moves a minuscule degree every time a frame of film is exposed.

ANIMATOR ANTHONY SCOTT hadn't seen such a high level of commitment to quality on the other stop-motion projects he had been involved with. "Usually, [the director] gives you your bit and says, 'Just go for it,'" Scott said.

"Programming the mocon is an interesting synthesis between left brain and right brain," Director of Photography Pete Kozachik said. "You have to know what the bits and bytes are doing, but you also have to have a feel for the quality of the shot." Even with a 1990 state-of-the-art motion control setup, some of the moves had to be done in the time-honored, hands-on way, especially for the simpler pans and tilts common in moviemaking.

For stop-motion, the camera position for each frame was figured out by determining the length of a shot. Then, a long piece of notched tape was placed along the camera's route, where each notch represented one frame. The camera was moved forward one notch after each shot. To further guarantee a smooth shot, many animators used a video frame-storer that enabled them to better keep track of things.

"With this system, I can flip between the previous two frames I shot and the current frame I'm working on . . . and make sure everything is moving in the right direction," Animator Owen Klatte said. "Sometimes I draw lines directly on the video screen, an outline of the character, so I can see over the course of, say, twenty frames, how the increments have changed."

On *Tim Burton's The Nightmare Before Christmas*, before doing the actual take (also known as the "hero shot"), four or five tests were done, shooting one frame for every ten or twenty frames to test the blocking and lighting and to tease out any problems that could arise. The test shots were invaluable because, unlike cel animation, mistakes on stop-motion can't be fixed by redrawing one frame. The scene starts on frame one and moves forward until the performance ends—no changes during the action are possible.

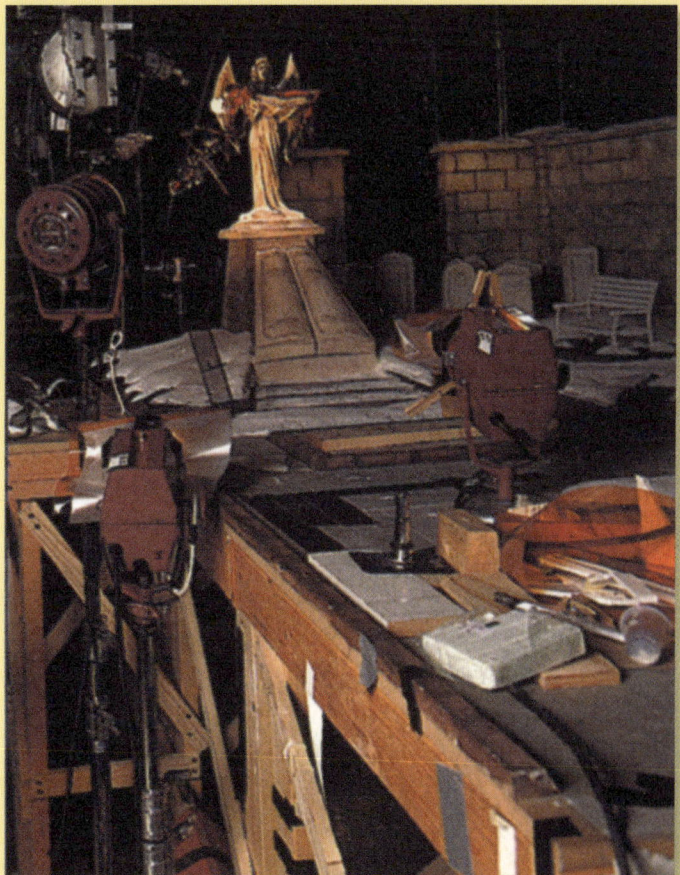

The animators were happy and grateful for the permission to experiment and the freedom of time to get it right. It resulted in a shared feeling of personal pride and a real sense of accomplishment borne out by the fact that the seventy-six minutes of animation in the final film is comprised of some 102,240 individual frames. It was that kind of commitment to the craft that made a masterpiece.

DR. FINKELSTEIN (CONT'D)
We need to be patient, that's all.

SALLY
But I don't want to be patient.

EXT. WILDERNESS - NIGHT

Jack walks glumly through the dark, tangled brush of the
wilderness, camera dollying with him.

Zero barks.

Zero enters, then flies playfully after Jack. Jack waves his
hand dismissingly at Zero.

JACK
No, Zero. Not now. I'm not in the mood.

Zero scoots in front of Jack and turns toward him.

Zero barks.

Camera holds as Jack stops, then looks at Zero with
resignation.

JACK (CONT'D)
All right.

Jack takes a bone out of his jacket.

JACK (CONT'D)
Here you go, boy.

Jack tosses the bone out of frame. Zero flies after the bone.
Zero flies through the air as he searches for the bone beside
some branches. Zero's nose lights up red and illuminates the
bone, which is beside a tree.

Zero barks.

Zero grabs the bone between his teeth, then flies and exits
with it. Jack walks glumly as Zero flies after him.

EXT. HALLOWEEN TOWN STREET - DAY

The saxophone player and the bass player, two members of the skeleton band, sleep. Jack's tower is through a gate. It is composed of a stone staircase which leads up to a house on a platform, which is constructed with extreme angles.

The saxophone player and bass player snore.

The Mayor enters in his hearse, then he stops the hearse. The Mayor steps out of the hearse, then he waves at the saxophone player and the bass player.

MAYOR
(optimistic face)

Mornin', gents.

BASS PLAYER

Uh-huh.

The Mayor, who is carrying plans and blueprints, turns and walks through the gate in front of Jack's house.

The Mayor hums "This is Halloween."

EXT. JACK'S TOWER - DAY

Looking down the staircase to the Mayor, who hurries up the stairs. The bass player and the saxophone player enter as they walk up to the bottom of the staircase. The Mayor pulls on the doorbell, which is made out of a spider on the end of a chain. The Mayor looks impatiently at the door, but there is no answer. The bass player and the saxophone player stand at the bottom of the staircase. The Mayor waves at the band members, then he turns and again pulls the doorbell.

MAYOR
(optimistic face)

Jack? You home?

There is still no answer. The Mayor's face suddenly spins and changes to its pessimistic face. The Mayor knocks against the door of Jack's tower. His face spins and returns to its optimistic face.

MAYOR (CONT'D)
(optimistic face)

Jack?!

The Mayor unfurls one of the rolled-up plans.

MAYOR (CONT'D)
(optimistic face)

I've got the plans for next Halloween. I need to go over
them with you so we can get started.

The Mayor switches to his pessimistic face as he gestures at
the door.

MAYOR (CONT'D)
(pessimistic face)

Jack, please. I'm only an elected official here. I can't
make decisions by myself.

The Mayor pulls out a megaphone and calls out toward the
tower.

MAYOR (CONT'D)
(pessimistic face)

Jack? Answer meeee!

The Mayor waves his hands at the door. The skeleton band
stands at the bottom of the staircase. The Mayor loses his
balance and tumbles down the staircase.

The Mayor screams.

The Mayor tumbles to the bottom of the staircase and smashes
against the gate. Low angle, past the Mayor, and through
the gate to the bass player, the saxophone player and the
accordion player, who look at him.

ACCORDION PLAYER

He's not home.

The Mayor looks up plaintively at the skeleton band.

MAYOR
(pessimistic face)

Where is he?

SCORING A FILM

Danny Elfman has composed dozens of scores for films over his remarkably successful career. Before he worked on *Tim Burton's The Nightmare Before Christmas*, he typically used a hundred or so musicians to create the grand, sweeping orchestrations that had become the hallmark of his career. But on this film, Elfman used an orchestra half that size in order to achieve his goal of creating a different, yet nostalgically familiar, musical score. "I wanted a punchy, old-fashioned sound on this," he said. "I wanted it to sound, even though it's in stereo, as if it were recorded in 1951."

Although Elfman could not score *Nightmare* until the film was edited together, the ten songs he had written before production began already filled about thirty minutes, or almost half, of the seventy-six minute movie, which gave him a good head start. And, importantly, the original songs also provided the musical core of the film.

"There was so much thematic material already there, that creating significant new thematic material would have been a detriment to the film," Elfman said. "The main problem was choosing which material I wanted to rely on most heavily for the score."

                         SAXOPHONE PLAYER
             He hasn't been home all night.

The Mayor's head falls to the ground with despair.

The Mayor groans.

EXT. WILDERNESS - DUSK

Looking through the trees to the sun, which is beginning to set.
Jack, who is exhausted, walks through the forest, camera dollying
with him, as Zero follows him. Jack rubs his skull.

                              JACK
                            (yawns)
             Where are we?

Camera dollies in toward the grove of trees. Jack walks through
the woods, camera dollying with him as he looks around at the
trees.

                         JACK (CONT'D)
             It's someplace new.

Jack walks as Zero floats along behind him. Jack exits, then Zero
stops and barks at him.

Zero barks.

Jack walks into the grove of trees, camera dollying back with him.

                         JACK (CONT'D)
             What is this?

A tree trunk stands in the grove with a heart-shaped door on
it. Camera dollies off the tree with the heart to reveal a tree
with a shamrock painted on it. Jack turns and looks around the
grove of trees. Camera dollies past the tree with the Easter egg
on it, to reveal the tree with the Thanksgiving turkey painted on
it. Jack looks thoughtfully at the Thanksgiving turkey. He then
turns and looks at the tree with the Christmas tree painted on it.
Jack reacts with surprise.

                         JACK (CONT'D)
             Huh.

Jack stares at the Christmas tree. Camera dollies in as Jack walks toward the Christmas tree. The doorknob on the Christmas tree, which is shaped like a Christmas tree bulb, shows a reflection of Jack, who walks toward the tree. Jack's hand enters and he grabs the doorknob. Jack opens the Christmas tree door on the tree, then he peers inside the tree. Jack turns as Zero enters, then Zero floats to a stop beside Jack. A winter wind suddenly blows up out of the tree. Jack looks around with surprise. The wind suddenly blows up into a blizzard force.

                    JACK (CONT'D)
     Whoooa!

Jack is sucked down into the tree, then the door slams shut after him.

Zero barks at the tree.

INT. CHRISTMAS TREE - DUSK

Camera spins down through a swirling vortex.

                    JACK
     Whoooooa!

Jack enters and falls through the vortex. White light floods the screen and obscures Jack.

EXT. CHRISTMAS LAND - NIGHT

Jack, sitting in the snow and rubbing his head, spins to a stop. Camera dollies in as Jack shakes his head, then stares at Christmas Town with delight. Camera dollies in toward Christmas Town, where every tree is a Christmas tree and every house is decorated with bright Christmas lights. Jack kneels in the snow and peers at Christmas Town. Jack momentarily loses his balance, causing him to look down at the snow. Jack lifts up some snow in his hand, then he eats some of it. Jack smiles, then he looks back at Christmas Town. A toy train moves across a striped trestle. Some tiny elves ice skate in a circle around a Christmas tree. Camera dollies in as Jack peers down at Christmas Town. Jack loses his balance. Jack slides down the side of the hill, camera dollying with him as he slides inside a snowdrift and is obscured. Jack reenters as his head pops out of the snow.

And the nightmares
cant be found

2A

One of the most critical elements of Tim Burton's The Nightmare Before Christmas *was the art of Tim Burton. While writing the original poem, Burton was also making sketches. His initial graphic look ultimately defined the production design for the film. Art Director Deane Taylor recalled what his charge was when he was hired. "My brief was, 'Make it look like Tim did it,'" Taylor said. "Luckily, the whole art department was in sync with . . . the visual language created by Tim's art."*

WHAT'S THIS?

What's this? What's this?
There's color everywhere
What's this?
There's white things in the air
What's this?
I can't believe my eyes
I must be dreaming
Wake up, Jack, this isn't fair
What's this?

What's this? What's this?
There's something very wrong
What's this?
There's people singing songs.
What's this?
The streets are lined with
Little creatures laughing
Everybody seems so happy
Have I possibly gone daffy?
What is this?

What's this?
There's children throwing snowballs
Instead of throwing heads
They're busy building toys
And absolutely no one's dead

There's frost in every window
Oh, I can't believe my eyes
And in my bones I feel a warmth
That's coming from inside

Oh, look, what's this?
They're hanging mistletoe. They kiss?
Why, that looks so unique. Inspired.
They're gathering around to hear a story
Roasting chestnuts on a fire
What's this?

"THE NIGHTMARE BEFORE CHRISTMAS" Set#9"Shot#14 song- "What's This?"

What's this? In here
They've got a little tree
How queer
And who would ever think, and why
They're covering it with tiny little things
They've got electric lights on strings
And there's a smile on everyone, so now
Correct me if I'm wrong
This looks like fun, this looks like fun
Oh, could it be I got my wish?
What's this?

Oh my, what now?
The children are asleep
But look, there's nothing underneath
No ghouls, no witches here to scream and scare them
Or ensnare them, only little cozy things
Secure inside their dreamland

What's this?
The monsters are all missing
And the nightmares can't be found
And in their place there seems to be
Good feeling all around

Instead of screams, I swear I can hear
Music in the air
The smell of cakes and pies
Are absolutely everywhere

The sights, the sounds
They're everywhere and all around
I've never felt so good before
This empty place inside of me is filling up
I simply cannot get enough

I want it, oh, I want it, oh, I want it for my own
I've got to know, I've got to know
What is this place that I have found?
What is this?

Smile on everyo

correct me if I'm wrong . . .

BURTON & SELICK

When *Tim Burton's The Nightmare Before Christmas* was given the green light for production by The Walt Disney Studios, Tim Burton was already committed to making *Batman Returns* for Warner Bros. So, even though *Nightmare* was one of Burton's most personal projects, he put the responsibility of directing the film into the hands of Henry Selick, a man he called "the most brilliant stop-motion director around."

Burton and Selick first met when they were students at CalArts prior to Selick graduating in 1977. In 1982, while both were still working together as animators at Disney, Burton showed Selick his original poem and sketches, making Selick one of the few who were associated with *Nightmare* from its inception. By then, the two realized they were kindred spirits. Reflecting on being asked to direct *Nightmare*, Selick said, wryly, "I was chosen for the job because I'm from the same planet, if not the same neighborhood, as Tim."

Burton decided at the onset that his film would be shot in stop-motion animation, so it followed that he would choose the stop-motion director he considered to be the best of the best for his project. Recognized as a major artist in his own right, Selick's résumé following his years at Disney had focused on stop-motion and included directing several acclaimed short films, creating national television commercials, and doing on-air promos and short segments for a new cable music network. Selick had a reputation for being collaborative and was well known as a creative talent who expanded the boundaries of stop-motion while still honoring the art form's history and traditions—a perfect combination for the project. Burton had no qualms about handing *Nightmare* off to a director making his feature-film debut.

Tim Burton's The Nightmare Before Christmas was the most ambitious and complicated stop-motion film that had ever been produced. It would take advantage of the latest 1990s technology, but, at its core, it was to be built on the most basic of techniques—hands-on manipulation of hand-crafted puppets, physical props, and tabletop sets.

"There's an inherent charm as well as a certain reality to stop-motion that you can't get with any other form of filmmaking," Selick said. "We use real materials, real cloth, and real puppets bathed in real light. The effect is a bit like opening a pop-up book or finding a great illustration in a storybook that feels like you can reach in and touch it or fall right into it."

When *Nightmare* was given the go-ahead, San Francisco was the hub of stop-motion animation, and Selick had been living and working there since the early 1980s. Disney and Burton set up production for the film in July 1991 and decided to produce the movie in San Francisco in order to take advantage of the local talent pool. Over the course of the work, driven by Burton's inspiration and Selick's leadership, 150 artists and technicians and 100 specially trained camera operators were hired, along with puppet makers, set builders, mold and armature makers, sculptors, computer operators, and more. The work began in rented offices and a sound stage at Tippett Studio and would expand to fill nineteen soundstages with 230 sets and hundreds of individual puppets. The years of work they did was tedious, detailed, and painstaking and created a world that looked reality-based but could never exist in real life.

The collaboration between Burton and Selick worked well for both creatives. At first, Burton was concerned that Selick would have different artistic ideas and approaches that would challenge Burton's decade-long-held vision of the film, which would have made for a complicated working relationship. But those fears were quickly assuaged by the rapport the two men established and the abiding respect they had—not only for one another, but also the art form of stop-motion animation. Selick said Burton gave him "enormous freedom to make the film work." And, understanding Burton's deep attachment to the film, Selick made sure that the Burton touch was everywhere. "That's part of my job," Selick said.

Burton would travel to San Francisco to check in on the progress of *Nightmare* whenever he wasn't shooting his other projects. He loved being there with the talented crew of artists working on the film. "The level of artistry and detail was magical, truly magical, and I'd never felt that before," Burton said. But for most of the production, Selick would send Burton filmed pieces every week to look over. That process went on for the three years it took to shoot the film. "Each time I would see a shot, I would get this little rush of energy; it was so beautiful," Burton said.

Tim Burton's The Nightmare Before Christmas received critical acclaim and won numerous awards and nominations but, at the time, was a minor box office hit. Since its 1993 release, the film has become recognized more widely as a true masterpiece of stop-motion filmmaking. Over the years, the film's fan base has grown, helping *Nightmare* take its place as a holiday staple. Every Halloween season at Disney theme parks, the beloved Haunted Mansion attraction is turned into a *Nightmare* showcase with themed products. Burton's story has maintained its grip on the public's imagination across generations, a fact that makes Burton smile.

"What's most meaningful to me is when you hear that new kids, a couple of generations in, have the same kind of response," Burton said. "You can't put it into words. There's something primal . . . that they seem to get, which is great."

Yarn boy

too big for ?

SAN FRANCISCO STUDIOS

TIM BURTON'S AESTHETIC began evolving and taking shape when he was just a young boy. Like many kids, it was nourished by pop-culture influences, such as cartoons, horror movies, and commercial art. Later, after being awarded a scholarship to the California Institute of the Arts, his studies of art history and theory, still-life drawing, and an academic approach to animation made him a more well-rounded artist and strengthened his appreciation of German Expressionism. The experience also affirmed his love of doodling and sketching and his unique gift for combining the mundane with the macabre.

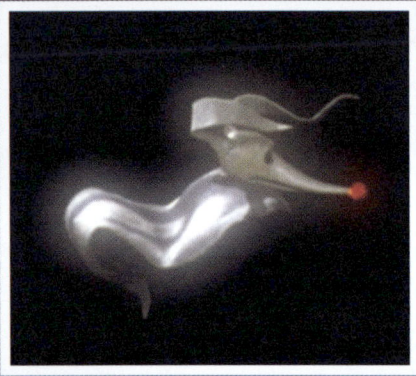

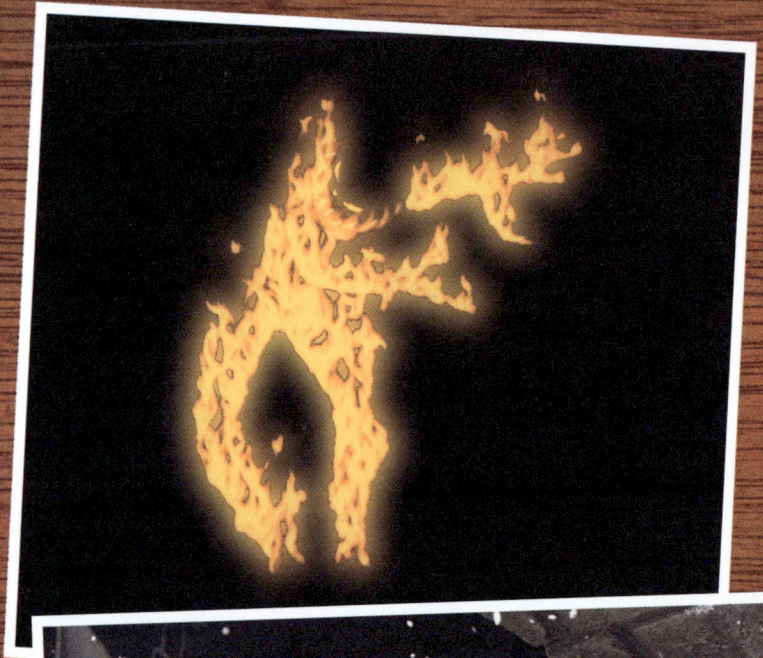

2-D EFFECTS

2-D special effects animation included things like ghosts, smoke, fire, snowflakes, shadows, and electricity, which added critical details and atmospherics to the story. For many scenes, the effects were added in post-production, and they had to interact seamlessly with the original stop-motion footage. Special Effects Animator Gordon Baker described the precision process: "I get a work print [of the finished scene], which has to be projected onto an animation stand and rotoscoped—traced frame-by-frame—so I can animate around the character."

On other occasions, Director Henry Selick, in an effort to be as true to the art and legacy of stop-motion animation as possible, would have the 2-D effects animation added during filming.

The guiding principle of effects production is that the work to get them onto the screen should never be noticed. For example, in the scene where Jack Skellington bursts into flame, the 2-D and 3-D animation were blended together to perfection. When Jack ignited the torch, real fire was used, but when the flame came near his mouth or moved over his body, the hand-drawn effects animation took over.

THE CELS USED in post-production were often executed in black and white. Color was added later with gels or by using an optical process.

Camera holds as Jack smashes into the candy cane signpost.
Jack falls into the snow, then he looks up at the signpost. A
sign is at the top of two candy cane signposts. The sign reads:
Christmas Town.

                          JACK
          Christmas Town?

Jack, sitting in the snow, looks up thoughtfully at the sign.

                      JACK (CONT'D)
          Hmmm.

Camera pans rapidly off Jack to reveal the factory. Camera
holds as a shadow of Santa Claus opening a door appears on a
snowbank.

                       SANTA CLAUS
                       (in shadow)
          Ho, ho, ho! Ho, ho, ho, ho . . .

Jack peers around the candy cane signpost at Santa Claus's
shadow.

                   SANTA CLAUS (CONT'D)
          . . . ho. Ho, ho, ho.

                          JACK
          Hmmm . . .

EXT. HALLOWEEN TOWN SQUARE - DAY

The Clown and Big Witch look at one another. Small Witch and
two vampires look at one another.

                          CLOWN
          This has never happened before.

                        BIG WITCH
          It's suspicious.

                       SMALL WITCH
          It's peculiar.

```
                    VAMPIRES
                  (in unison)
      It's scary.

The Mayor pushes past the Wolfman
and the Behemoth.

                    MAYOR
                (pessimistic face)
      Stand aside. Coming through.

The Wolfman growls.

The Mayor steps to his hearse. The Mayor then climbs up a
ladder to the top of his hearse. The Mayor stumbles and falls
down on the roof of the hearse.

The Mayor groans.

The Mayor stands up and picks up a megaphone off the roof. He
looks at the creatures.

                    MAYOR (CONT'D)
          (pessimistic face) (into megaphone)
We've got to find Jack. There's only three hundred and sixty-five
days left till next Halloween.

The Wolfman holds up four fingers toward the Mayor.

                    WOLFMAN
      Three sixty-four!

                    MAYOR
          (pessimistic face) (into microphone)
      Is there anywhere we've forgotten to check?

                    CLOWN
                  (chuckling)
      I looked in every mausoleum.

                BIG WITCH & SMALL WITCH
                    (in unison)
      We opened the sarcophagi.
```

MR. HYDE
I tromped through the pumpkin patch.

VAMPIRE
I peeked behind the cyclops' eye.

The vampire pulls out his eyeball and demonstrates.

VAMPIRE (CONT'D)
I did. But he wasn't there.

The Mayor looks frantically at the creatures.

MAYOR
(pessimistic face) (into microphone)
It's time to sound the alarms.

The mummy, standing on the hood of the hearse, cranks a siren, which is formed in the shape of a metal cat.

EXT. DR. FINKELSTEIN'S HOME - DAY

Camera dollies in toward Dr. Finkelstein's home, which is a huge tower on top of a mound.

INT. DR. FINKELSTEIN'S HOME/KITCHEN - DAY

Sally stands at a window and listens to the sound of the siren. Sally turns and walks across the kitchen. A jar sits on a shelf inside a cabinet. The lettering on the jar reads: deadly nightshade. The cabinet doors open to reveal Sally, who reaches and grabs the jar. Sally takes the jar, then she turns and looks thoughtfully at it. Sally walks, camera dollying with her to reveal a bubbling cauldron. Camera holds as Sally pours the nightshade into the cauldron. The form of a skull's head appears in the fumes coming out of the cauldron. Sally covers her nose.

Sally groans.

Sally lowers her hands, then she reaches and takes a can of frog's breath off a shelf.

VAMPIRE:
I peeked behind the Cyclops' eye.   (7AREV)

SALLY
Frog's breath'll overpower any odor.

Sally opens the lid of the can, then a frog pokes his head
up out of the can. Sally holds the can above the cauldron.
The frog opens his mouth and exhales his smoky breath into
the cauldron.

Sally groans.

Sally holds her nose and lowers the can of frog's breath
out of frame.

Sally coughs. Sally, who is is overcome by the fumes of the
frog's breath, staggers across the kitchen.

SALLY (CONT'D)
(sneezes)
Bitter.

SALLY (CONT'D)
(coughs and gasps)
Worm's wort.

Sally staggers and opens a cabinet, then she tosses bottles
as she searches for the worm's wort.

SALLY (CONT'D)
Where's that worm's wort?

Sally lifts a bottle of worm's wort out of the cabinet. Sally
stares at the bottle of worm's wort.

Dr. FINKELSTEIN (OFF)
Sally?

Sally looks up at the sound of Dr. Finkelstein's voice.

DR. FINKELSTEIN (OFF) (CONT'D)
That soup ready yet?

Sally pours the worm's wort into the cauldron. Sally sniffs
the soup.

TRY TO maintain the asymmetry of the dress in this drawing while keeping it close enough to her waist so that when animators grab her there it doesn't shift.

Sally has sewn her dress together from found fabric ~~garments piece~~ sections.

← 3-D STICHES ·LIKE HER SKIN HAS.

dress should be made out of a material that <u>can</u> be animated for secondary action or effect, but doesn't have to respond to every move she makes. (CONSULT ERIC)

SALLY'S DRESS

call me with any questions – Rick

VISUAL CONSULTANT RICK HEINRICHS worked with the writer and animators to redesign the Sally puppet. In this concept drawing, Heinrichs has provided specific production notes for Bonita DeCarlo and her team of character fabricators.

CHARACTER CREATION

Everything about the design of the puppets was painstakingly crafted. That exacting process included wardrobes for more than sixty characters comprised of fabrics, furs, foam, latex, notions, and paints. While some characters had their clothing painted on, main characters like Jack and Sally had separate wardrobe pieces. One of the more involved pieces of wardrobe was Sally's dress.

"The first step was to have a dress sculpted for the puppet's body," explained Character Fabricator Supervisor Bonita DeCarlo. "That was then molded and cast in foam latex to provide a surface to lay the [cotton Lycra®] dress onto. The dress itself [had] a silkscreened pattern that has been hand-painted, laid onto foam, and carefully stitched."

Sally's garment had to be realistic and sturdy. "When Sally walks or lifts her leg, the dress moves with her," DeCarlo said. Sally was replicated so animators could work with her in several scenes simultaneously. The puppets had to be made to stand up to the rigors of animation. Even the paint used was strengthened with polymers to resist scratching, denting, and breaking while still retaining flexibility.

"The process of animation is very rough on the puppets, so the stronger we make the paint job, the better the puppet will hold up through a number of shots," DeCarlo explained.

SALLY

   Ah.

Sally smiles, then she looks up in the direction of Dr. Finkelstein.

SALLY (CONT'D)

   Coming!

INT. DR. FINKELSTEIN'S HOUSE/LABORATORY - DAY

Looking across a table to Dr. Finkelstein, who sits in his
wheelchair and peers down through a microscope. Dr. Finkelstein
pulls his head away from the microscope, then opens the top of his
skull to reveal his brain. Dr. Finkelstein rubs his brain as he
thinks. Sally, carrying a bowl of soup, enters, then she stops and
looks at Dr. Finkelstein.

SALLY

   Lunch!

Dr. Finkelstein swings his wheelchair around and closes his skull.
Sally sets the bowl of soup down on the table.

DR. FINKELSTEIN

   Ah. What's that?

Dr. Finkelstein sniffs the soup.

DR. FINKELSTEIN (CONT'D)
(inhales)

   Worm's wort! Mmm.

Dr. Finkelstein scoops a spoonful of soup out of the bowl and
sniffs it.

DR. FINKELSTEIN (CONT'D)
(inhales)

   And frog's breath.

Dr. Finkelstein suddenly glares at Sally. She backs out of frame.
Looking over the table, with the bowl of soup on it, to Sally, who
backs away. She then gestures at Dr. Finkelstein.

SALLY
   What's wrong? I thought you liked frog's breath.

Dr. Finkelstein leans in and glares at Sally.

                    DR. FINKELSTEIN
          Nothing's more suspicious than frog's breath. Until you
          taste it, I won't swallow a spoonful.

Dr. Finkelstein slides the bowl across the table toward Sally.
Dr. Finkelstein's hand holds a spoonful of the soup toward Sally,
who looks nervously at it. Sally swings her hand, which knocks
against Dr. Finkelstein's hand.

                    SALLY
          I'm not hungry.

The spoon falls to the floor.

                    SALLY (CONT'D)
          Oops.

Dr. Finkelstein leans back in his wheelchair and looks at Sally
with exaggerated concern.

                    DR. FINKELSTEIN
          You want me to starve.

Sally reaches down to the spoon on the floor, then she slides
the spoon under the table.

                    DR. FINKELSTEIN (CONT'D)
          An old man like me, who hardly has strength as it is.

Sally pulls a slotted spoon out from inside her sock.

                    DR. FINKELSTEIN (CONT'D)
          Me! To whom you owe your very life.

                    SALLY
          Oh, don't be silly!

Sally reaches toward the bowl of soup, which is on the table, and
lifts it toward herself. Sally puts the slotted spoon down in the
soup, but the soup just runs out of the slots. Camera moves past
Dr. Finkelstein to Sally, who lifts the slotted spoon and pretends
to slurp the soup.

                    SALLY (CONT'D)
                    (slurps soup)
     Mmm. See? Scrumptious.

Sally lowers the bowl of soup onto the table. Past Sally, standing
and putting the bowl of soup down on the table, to Dr. Finkelstein,
who sits in his wheelchair and looks thoughtfully at Sally.
Dr. Finkelstein looks down excitedly at the bowl of soup. Dr.
Finkelstein lifts the bowl of soup and begins to drink from it.
Sally smiles at Dr. Finkelstein.

Dr. Finkelstein slurps soup.

EXT. HALLOWEEN TOWN SQUARE - DUSK

The Mayor, with his pessimistic face turned, lies atop his hearse
and stares up despairingly at the sky. The vampires sit on the
running board of the hearse and the witches sit in the cab.

                    MAYOR
                    (pessimistic face)
          Did anyone think to dredge the lake?

                    VAMPIRE
                    (sighs)
     This morning.

                    ZERO (OFF)
                    (barks)

Small Witch, sitting in the hearse driver's seat, looks at Big Witch,
who sits in the passenger seat.

                    BIG WITCH
     Hear that?

                    SMALL WITCH
     What?

Big Witch takes off her hat so that she can hear more clearly.

                    BIG WITCH
     Shh.

Zero barks.

The Mayor sits up as he hears Zero barking, then the Mayor's
head turns to his optimistic face. One of the vampires stands up.

                    ANOTHER VAMPIRE
          Zero.

Looking through a barred gate to Zero, who enters and flies
between the bars in the gate.

Zero barks.

Jack enters driving a Christmas Town snowmobile toward the
gate. A huge bag, filled with Christmas memorabilia, is on the
snowmobile. The bars on the gate open and Jack drives through
the gate.

          (Overlapping, indistinct excited chatter and
           cheering continues under following scene)

                         KID
          Jack's back!

Zero flies and exits. Camera cranes down as some creatures enter
and excitedly greet Jack. Jack drives the snowmobile across the
town square, camera dollying with him, to reveal the Mayor, who
stands atop the hearse. Creatures run excitedly alongside the
snowmobile.

                        MAYOR
                   (optimistic face)
          Where have you been?

High angle past the Mayor, standing on the roof of the hearse,
to Jack, who sits in the snowmobile and gestures at him.

                        JACK
          Call a town meeting and I'll tell everyone all about it.

The Mayor's face switches to its pessimistic side. The Mayor
stares down at Jack.

                              MAYOR
                        (pessimistic face)
          When?

                              JACK

          Immediately!

Camera dollies back as a bell in the Town Hall tower rings.

EXT. HALLOWEEN TOWN - DUSK

The Mayor, whose optimistic face is turned forward, drives his
hearse, camera dollying with him.

                              MAYOR
                (optimistic face) (into microphone)
          Town meeting! Town meeting! Town meeting tonight!

Camera moves off of the Mayor's hearse and tilts up to reveal
Dr. Finkelstein's house.

INT. DR. FINKELSTEIN'S HOUSE /LABORATORY - NIGHT

Sally leans toward Dr. Finkelstein, who sits in his wheelchair
and sleeps against the table. Sally lays a shawl over his
shoulders.

Dr. Finkelstein snores.

                              MAYOR
                        (over speaker)
          Town meeting! Town meeting tonight!

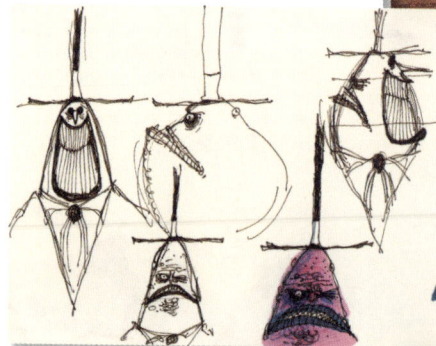

Sally hurries and exits.

EXT. TOWN HALL - NIGHT

Sally walks up the front steps to the Town Hall. Other
creatures move toward the Town Hall.

Small Witch enters on her broom and swoops toward the Town Hall. Small Witch yells indistinctly.

Sally steps and lets Small Witch fly past her and exit into the Town Hall.

INT. TOWN HALL - NIGHT

Creatures take their seats and face toward the stage. Sally enters, then walks backwards as she gapes at the creatures in the crowded Town Hall.

> (Overlapping, low and indistinct chatter
> continues under following scenes and dialogue)

The Clown enters and moves on a unicycle, bumping into Sally.

                    SALLY
     Oh!

The Clown chuckles.

Sally steps right as the clown cycles down the main aisle. A door opens and Jack enters. He walks across the stage, camera dollying slightly with him to reveal a podium. Jack stands behind the podium and gestures at the creatures.

                    JACK
     Listen, everyone.

Some creatures take their seats and look at Jack. The lights dim.

                    JACK (CONT'D)
     I want to tell you about Christmas Town.

The Mayor, with his optimistic face turned forward, turns on a spotlight and aims it at Jack. Camera dollies in as Jack, standing in the spotlight, looks at the creatures.

TOWN MEETING SONG

There are objects so peculiar
They were not to be believed
All around things to tantalize my brain
It's a world unlike anything I've ever seen
And hard as I tried I can't seem to describe
Like a most improbable dream
But you must believe when I tell you this
It's as real as my skull and it does exist
Here, let me show you
This is a thing called a present
The whole thing starts with a box

A box?
Is it steel?
Are there locks?
Is it filled with a pox?
A pox. How delightful, a pox.

If you please
Just a box, with bright colored paper
And the whole thing's topped with a bow

A bow?
But why?
How ugly
What's in it? What's in it?

That's the point of the thing, not to know

It's a bat
Will it bend?
It's a rat
Will it break?
Perhaps it's the head that I found in the lake

Listen now, you don't understand
That's not the point of Christmas Land
Now pay attention
We pick up an oversized sock
And hang it like this on the wall

Oh, yes. Does it still have a foot?
Let me see. Let me look.
Is it rotted and covered with gook?

Um, let me explain
There's no foot inside, but there's candy
Or sometimes it's filled with small toys

Small toys?
Do they bite?
Do they snap?
Or explode in the sack?
Or perhaps they just spring out and scare girls and boys

What a splendid idea
This Christmas sounds fun
I fully endorse it
Let's try it at once

Everyone, please, now not so fast
There's something here that you don't quite grasp
Well, I may as well give them what they want
And the best, I must confess, I have saved for the last
For the ruler of this Christmas Land
Is a fearsome king with a deep mighty voice
Least that's what I've come to understand

And I've also heard it told
That he's something to behold
Like a lobster, huge and red
When he sets out to slay with his rain gear on
Carting bulging sacks with his big great arms
That is, so I've heard it said

And on a dark cold night
Under full moonlight,
He flies into a fog
Like a vulture in the sky
And they call him Sandy Claws

Well, at least they're excited
But they don't understand
That special kind of feeling in Christmas Land
Oh, well

STORYBOARDS

Pinning up story sketches on 4x8-foot bulletin boards to create storyboards was an innovation created by the Walt Disney Story department in the 1930s. At that time, the studio was releasing about twenty-four cartoon shorts a year, and keeping all the notes and story drawings straight was a challenge. Story man and animator Webb Smith is credited by Disney with coming up with the idea of putting those drawings onto a bulletin board in sequence, side by side, row by row. Not only did it allow a large group to see the flow of the story, it also made it easy to add or replace drawings or to revise the story simply by replacing or reorganizing the storyboard panels. Storyboarding was first used to its full extent on the 1933 classic cartoon *Three Little Pigs*. Since that time, its use has become ubiquitous throughout the film industry and beyond.

Like most elements of this film's production, storyboarding did not follow the traditional route of an animated film. Since the songs were written before the script, the artists began storyboarding them first. "What's This?" was the first song to be boarded shot-by-shot for the film. Working from Danny Elfman's song and Tim Burton's original sketches and drawings, the storyboard artists added comedic bits and gags, such as Jack bumping into, then jumping inside of, a snowman. According to Head Storyboard Artist Joe Ranft, this approach of starting with the songs worked well for them because, "Danny Elfman's songs are like miniature films in themselves," he said.

When writer Caroline Thompson's script was completed, the storyboard artists were able to map out the entire film. Creating the original boards required a constant flow of ideas between the artists, the writer, Visual Consultant Rick Heinrichs, and Director Henry Selick—along with input from Burton. Thompson would make script changes based on the artist's input and send the new draft back. The artists would then make their adjustments in rough-draft form. The exchanges continued until each scene felt right. Selick would give a thumbs up or down on the scene, and the artists would move on to the actual task of storyboarding based on his notes and recommendations.

Some fifty storyboards were done for the film, with about sixty-six drawings in each of them. Completing the original storyboards took between eight and twelve months, according to Ranft. When a storyboarded scene was complete, the drawings were then shot and edited together with a running time equal to what would appear in the film. The sequence was also synced up to a dialogue soundtrack. As scenes were animated, they were added into the storyboard reel, replacing the storyboard images until the scenes were complete.

The importance of storyboards went beyond providing guidance for shot composition. Every department relied on them in one way or another. The lighting department plotted their lighting based on the boards. Set builders, prop makers, puppet fabricators, sculptors, special effects animators, and even facilities managers who had to assign the physical workspace relied on the storyboards. As any animator knows, clear and precise storyboards save time, money, and frustration, especially on a film as complicated and detail laden as *Tim Burton's The Nightmare Before Christmas*.

J: WHAT IS THIS? (10)

Jack comes forward

TO What This

J: WHERE ARE WE? (3c)

STORYBOARDS ARE THE FIRST VISUAL VERSION of a movie, showing the scenes of the story through a series of drawings that can be either very rough or extremely detailed. But storyboard panels portray much more than the action taking place in a scene. They also give information about staging, props, camera angles, and movement.

EXT. JACK'S TOWER - NIGHT

Camera dollies in on Jack's tower.

INT. JACK'S TOWER - NIGHT

Jack sits by the fireplace and reads a book. Other books are laid
on the bed. The title on the book cover reads: Santa's Workshop.

                         JACK
          Hm.

Jack closes his book and puts it down, then he picks up another
book and looks through it. The title on the book cover reads:
A Christmas Carol. Jack puts the book down, then he picks up
another book and browses through it. The title on the book reads:
Rudolph.

                    JACK (CONT'D)
          Hm.

Camera holds as Jack closes the book, then he looks up
thoughtfully. Camera dollies along a string of Christmas lights
to reveal a huge spiderweb, which has been festooned with
Christmas lights. Camera tilts down to reveal Zero, who sleeps in
a basket under a Christmas tree. The lettering on Zero's food dish
reads: Zero. Jack points to his head thoughtfully.

                    JACK (CONT'D)
     There's got to be a logical way to explain this Christmas thing.

Jack reaches and lifts a book. Jack opens the book, the cover of
which reads: The Scientific Method. Camera dollies in on Jack, who
reads the book intently.

INT. DR. FINKELSTEIN'S HOME/CORRIDOR - DAY

Camera moves past Dr. Finkelstein, sitting in his wheelchair and
rubbing his head, through a doorway to Sally, who sits on her bed
and stares down glumly at the floor.

                    DR. FINKELSTEIN
     You've poisoned me for the last time, you wretched girl.

Dr. Finkelstein slams the bedroom door shut, obscuring Sally. A bar drops down into place across the door. Dr. Finkelstein rubs his head.

Dr. Finkelstein moans.

The doorbell rings.

>   DR. FINKELSTEIN (CONT'D)
>   Oh, my head.

Dr. Finkelstein drives his wheelchair toward a balcony.

>   DR. FINKELSTEIN (CONT'D)
>   The door is open.

Camera continues to dolly in over the balcony and tilts down to reveal the front door, which opens to reveal Jack. Jack steps into the house and looks around.

>   JACK
>   Hello?

>   DR. FINKELSTEIN
>   Jack Skellington!

INT. DR. FINKELSTEIN'S HOUSE/SALLY'S ROOM - DAY

Sally, hearing Jack's name, sits up straight on her bed and smiles.

>   DR. FINKELSTEIN
>   Up here, my boy.

INT. DR. FINKELSTEIN'S HOUSE/FOYER - DAY

Past Jack to Dr. Finkelstein, who sits on the upper floor balcony and looks down at him.

>   JACK
>   Doctor, I need to borrow some equipment.

Jack walks up the circular staircase toward Dr. Finkelstein.

>   DR. FINKELSTEIN
>   Is that so? Whatever for?

Jack, who is carrying a satchel, walks up to the top of the staircase. Jack stops and looks at Dr. Finkelstein.

                         JACK
          I'm conducting a series of experiments.

                         DR. FINKELSTEIN
          How perfectly marvelous. Curiosity killed the cat, you
know.

                         JACK
          I know.

                         DR. FINKELSTEIN
          Come on into the lab . . .

Dr. Finkelstein turns his wheelchair around and drives it.

                         DR. FINKELSTEIN (CONT'D)
          . . . and we'll get you all fixed up.

Jack follows Dr. Finkelstein.

INT. DR. FINKELSTEIN'S HOUSE/SALLY'S ROOM - DAY

Sally leans against the door and listens intently.

                         SALLY
          Hmm. Experiments?

INT. JACK'S TOWER - DAY

Zero sleeps in his basket.

                         JACK
          Zero! I'm home!

Zero wakes up and looks around. Jack walks up to the top of the staircase in his tower, then he sets his satchel down on a table. He opens the satchel to reveal test tubes, beakers, and other scientific equipment, which are inside it. Jack arranges the test tubes and beakers on the table, then he picks up a microscope. Jack's hands put the microscope down on the table.

Some berries are on a sprig of mistletoe. Jack's hand reaches in and takes one of the berries. Jack places the berry on a glass slide and puts it under the microscope. Jack looks at the berry through the microscope. Looking through the telescope to the berry, which is on the slide, Jack moves the lens down, which crushes the berry against the slide. Jack leans down and looks at the berry with dismay.

INT. JACK'S TOWER - A SHORT TIME LATER

Jack has attached a battery to some beakers. He drops a candy cane into one of the beakers, then some red smoke comes out of the beaker. Jack uses tongs to pull the candy cane out of the beaker. The candy cane has lost its stripes. Jack stares at the candy cane quizzically.

INT. JACK'S TOWER - A SHORT TIME LATER

Jack sits in a chair at his desk and folds a piece of paper in half. A slide of a snowflake is on the right. Jack starts to cut the piece of paper into the shape of a snowflake. However, when Jack opens the paper, the paper is cut in the shape of a spider, not a snowflake. Jack stares at the paper with surprise.

INT. JACK'S TOWER - A SHORT TIME LATER

Jack looks at a teddy bear, which lays on an operating table. Jack uses a scalpel to cut open the teddy bear's stomach. Cotton stuffing comes out of the teddy bear. Jack uses some tweezers to lift the cotton out of the teddy bear's stomach. Jack straightens up, camera tilting up with him, off the teddy bear. Jack lifts a magnifying glass into frame and peers through it at the cotton stuffing. Camera dollies in on the magnifying glass.

INT. JACK'S TOWER - NIGHT

Zero sleeps in his basket as a Christmas tree bulb spins on the bottom of the Christmas tree. Jack's hand enters and he takes the bulb off the tree. Jack lifts the bulb above a beaker, filled with heated water. Jack crushes the Christmas bulb and lets the dust fall down into the beaker. The beaker starts to glow green.

                              JACK
          Interesting reaction.

Jack gestures at the beaker with frustration.

                          JACK (CONT'D)
          But what does it mean?

INT. DR. FINKELSTEIN'S HOUSE/SALLY'S ROOM - NIGHT

Camera looking through the barred window of Sally's room to Jack's
tower, where the green glow of the Christmas bulb is visible. Camera
dollies back to reveal Sally, who pours some potion into a bottle,
which is on a table. Other jugs and jars are on the table. Camera
holds as Sally glances at the door, then Sally scoops up some grains
out of a jar and puts them into the bottle. Sally puts a cork in the
bottle.

A basket sits beside Sally's sewing machine. Sally's hands enter and
put the bottle into the basket. Sally picks up the basket, which is
attached to the thread in the sewing machine, and exits with it.
Sally carries the basket as the sewing machine unspools the thread
behind it. Sally opens the window.

EXT. DR. FINKELSTEIN'S HOUSE - NIGHT

Looking through the window, as the bars swing open, to Sally, who
stands in her room. Sally lowers the basket to the ground. Sally
looks up at Jack's tower. The green light pulsates in the windows of
Jack's tower. Camera looking through the window to Sally, who smiles
at Jack's tower. Sally takes a deep breath, then she leaps through
the window and exits lower frame. Sally falls through the air. The
members of the skeleton band cringe as Sally hits the ground. They
then look at Sally. Sally lies on the ground, her legs and one of
her arms knocked off her torso. The basket is on the ground. Camera
cranes down and dollies in on Sally's head as her eyes open. Sally
pushes up on her arm. Sally, kneeling on the ground, looks up over
her shoulder at Dr. Finkelstein's house. Sally then reaches toward
her other arm. Sally's hand enters, then she pulls her other arm

out of frame. Sally pulls a sewing needle out from behind her ear. Sally pulls a spool of thread out from inside a pocket in her dress. Sally sews her arm back onto her torso. One of Sally's legs lays on the ground. Sally's hand enters, then she pulls the leg out of frame.

EXT. DR. FINKELSTEIN'S HOUSE - A SHORT TIME LATER

Sally sits on the ground and finishes sewing her second leg onto her torso. She puts the needle back behind her ear, then she reaches and picks up the basket. Sally stands up and walks. The skeleton band plays. Sally enters as she walks down some stairs, then she carries the basket past the band.

INT. DR. FINKELSTEIN'S HOUSE/SALLY'S ROOM - NIGHT

The door to Sally's room is closed.

                    DR. FINKELSTEIN (OFF)
          You can come out . . .

The door opens to reveal Dr. Finkelstein, who sits in his wheelchair. He drives into the room.

                    DR. FINKELSTEIN (CONT'D)
          . . . now if you promise to behave.

Dr. Finkelstein stops the wheelchair, then he holds up a lantern and looks around the room.

                    DR. FINKELSTEIN (CONT'D)
          Sally? Sally?!

Camera dollies in on Dr. Finkelstein, who reacts angrily as he realizes Sally is gone.

                    DR. FINKELSTEIN (CONT'D)
                         (growls)
          Gone again!

Dr. Finkelstein drops the lantern out of frame to the floor.

INT. JACK'S TOWER - NIGHT

Camera dollies across a chalkboard, the handwriting on which
reads: Sugar Plum Visions, Egg Nog x (chestnuts/open fire) /
bell [square root of 12 over Dec.25] + Sandy = Christmas?

Camera continues to dolly to reveal Jack, who finishes making
the question mark on the chalkboard. Jack looks at the
chalkboard, then he rubs his head thoughtfully. The basket is
visible through a window as Sally pulls it up on a rope.

                         JACK
          Hmm.

The basket swings and hits the window. Jack turns and looks
at the basket with surprise, then he opens the window. He looks
down at Sally.

EXT. JACK'S TOWER - NIGHT

Camera moves in on Sally, who stands on the ground and holds
the other end of the rope. Jack grabs hold of the basket, then
he waves down at Sally.

INT. JACK'S TOWER - NIGHT

Jack takes the basket off the rope, then he puts the basket
down on
the windowsill.

Jack's hands, reaching in from the left, slide a towel off the
top of the basket to reveal the bottle and the food. Jack lifts
the bottle and pulls out the cork. Fumes float out of the bottle
and form in the shape of a death's-head moth. Jack smiles as
the fumes dissipate. Jack walks to the window.

EXT. JACK'S TOWER - NIGHT

Camera looks through the window to Jack, who leans over and
looks
down for Sally. He reacts with surprise as he realizes she is
gone. The rope extends to the ground, but Sally is gone. Jack
leans out the window and peers down at the ground. He looks
around sadly, then he closes the window.

EXT. HALLOWEEN TOWN STREET - NIGHT

Sally closes the gate of Jack's tower, then she hides behind the front wall. She smiles dreamily and slides down to the ground. She reaches toward a bush with some flowers. Sally, sitting on the ground, pulls a flower off the bush. Sally smiles as she pulls petals off the flower. Suddenly the flower begins to wiggle and spin.

Sally gasps.

The flower starts to shake. Sally's hand, reaching in, holds the flower, which shakes. The flower suddenly transforms into a Christmas tree, with lights and Christmas ornaments hanging from the branches. A star appears on the top of the tree, then the Christmas tree bursts into flame.

Sally stares at the Christmas tree, which burns until it extinguishes. Smoke curls up from the withered branches. Camera dollies in slightly, off Sally, who continues to stare at the Christmas tree.

EXT. JACK'S TOWER - DAWN

A rooster sleeps on a rooftop as sunlight from the rising sun strikes him. The rooster wakes up and crows.

Rooster crows.

Four vampires sleep on the wall of Jack's tower as Sally sleeps curled up against the wall. The four vampires wake up.

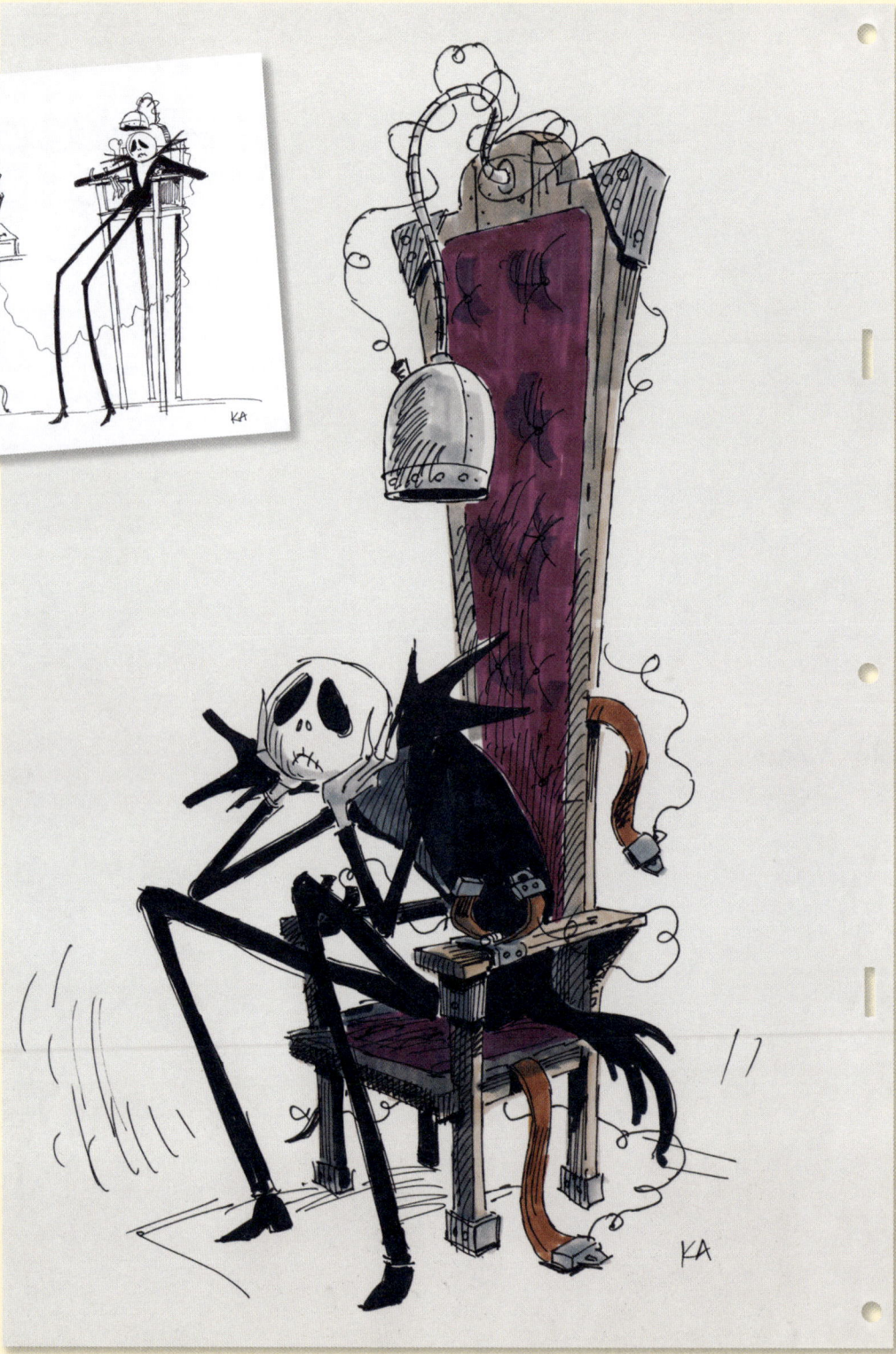

JACK'S OBSESSION

Something's up with Jack
Something's up with Jack
Don't know if we're ever going to get him back

He's all alone up there
Locked away inside
Never says a word
Hope he hasn't died
Something's up with Jack
Something's up with Jack

Christmastime is buzzing in my skull
Will it let me be? I cannot tell
There're so many things I cannot grasp
When I think I've got it then at last
Through my bony fingers it does slip
Like a snowflake in a fiery grip

Something here I'm not quite getting
Though I try, I keep forgetting
Like a memory long since past
Here in an instant, gone in a flash
What does it mean?
What does it mean?

In these little bric-a-brac
A secret's waiting to be cracked
These dolls and toys confuse me so,
Confound it all, I love it though

Simple objects, nothing more
But something's hidden through a door
Though I do not have the key
Something's here I cannot see
What does it mean?
What does it mean?

What does it mean?

I've read these Christmas books so many times
I know the stories and I know the rhymes
I know the Christmas carols all by heart
My skull's so full it's tearing me apart
As often as I've read them, something's wrong
So hard to put my bony finger on

Or perhaps it's really not as deep
As I've been led to think
Am I trying much too hard?
Of course! I've been too close to see
The answer's right in front of me!
Right in front of me!

It's simple really, very clear
Like music drifting in the air
Invisible, but everywhere
Just because I cannot see it
Doesn't mean I can't believe it

You know, I think this Christmas thing
Is not as tricky as it seems
And why should they have all the fun?
It should belong to anyone

Not anyone, in fact, but me
Why, I could make a Christmas tree
And there's no reason I can find
I couldn't handle Christmastime

I bet I could improve it, too
And that's exactly what I'll do

TRACK READER

Most of the puppets created for *Tim Burton's The Nightmare Before Christmas* had pliable mouths that the animators would manipulate by hand to create the illusion that the character was speaking. A few of the puppets had faces that could be popped off and replaced with another face fashioned with a different mouth position. That was true for the trio of trick-or-treaters Lock, Shock, and Barrel; the Mayor; and for Sally, who had a set of thirteen different faces.

But Jack was different. As the main character, he was outfitted with a large number of separate heads. There was a basic set of mouth movements, of course, but a full complement of those would be needed for each of Jack's moods, such as happy, sad, mad, or neutral. The sum of all those would be needed for each of the eighteen Jack puppets that would often be working on different sets at the same time. In all, as many as 400 distinctly different Jack heads were created. If for some reason a new head was needed, the sculpting and molding departments were on-site and on-call as needed.

It was critical during shooting that the animators knew exactly which replacement face or head to use for each frame. Track Reader Dan Mason's job began with breaking down the finished soundtrack into sounds that were charted across a timeline in increments of twenty-four frames per second. With those completed track sheets (also called exposure sheets) in hand, animators knew when to open and close the mouth for the consonants, vowels, and other sounds. Normally, that was where the track reader's job ended. But Mason, working with technicians, innovated a new process that expanded the role of a track reader and took it to a new level.

Using a state-the-art desktop computer, which, at the time, was an Apple Macintosh IIci, Mason uploaded photographs of all of a character's replacement heads or faces and programmed the computer to play back the dialogue and faces in sync at precisely twenty-four frames per second, the rate at which the film would be projected. Getting that all to work properly consumed about two months, Mason recalled.

Once the system was set up properly, Mason, working as a one-man department, began the process of matching every frame of dialogue with a numbered photograph of the head that had the corresponding mouth position. It was a laborious job.

"I would revise, and revise, and revise it," Mason said. When he felt everything was in place, he would run the line as a short movie and verify that the mouth movements and expressions were in sync with the dialogue.

The innovation met with mixed reaction among the animators. Mason was, in effect, animating the character's lip sync in the computer, a task that was traditionally solely in the hands of the animator. Some of *Nightmare*'s animators were happy with the process, seeing it as a real time saver that would give them more time to work on their character's acting. Others were ambivalent and preferred choosing some of the replacement heads themselves.

After making final changes, Mason printed out a "head script" that corresponded to the track sheet, which made the labor-intensive process of stop-motion animation more efficient and contributed to the overall success of the final film.

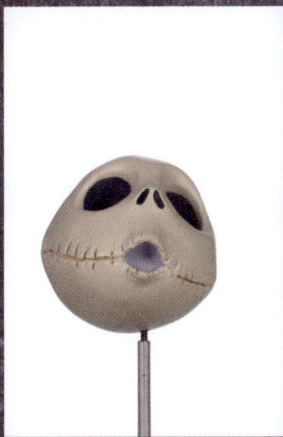

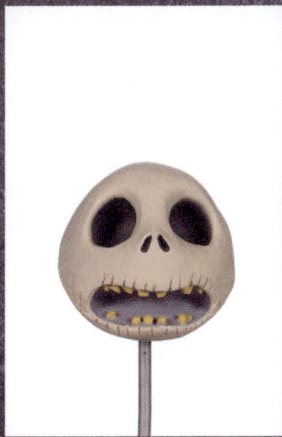

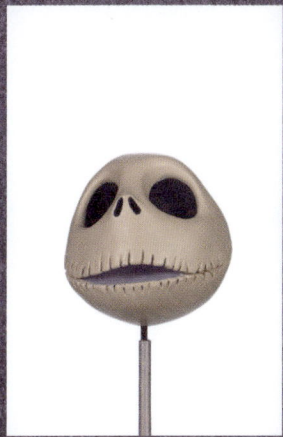

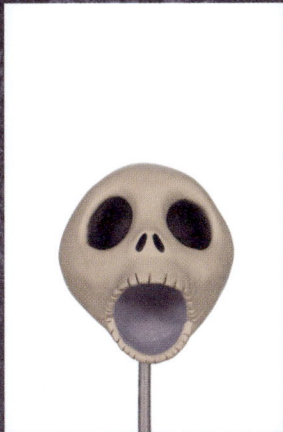

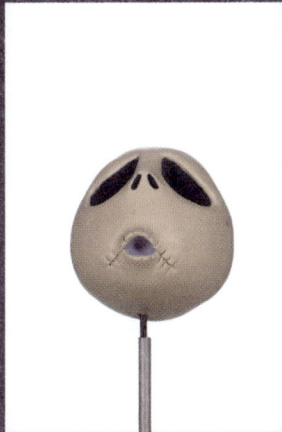

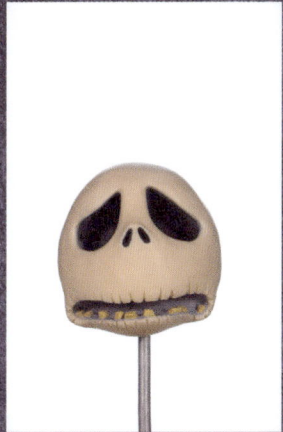

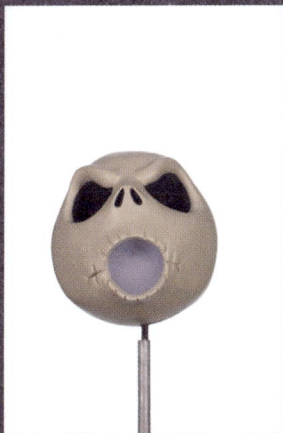

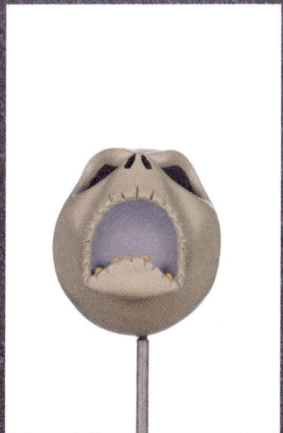

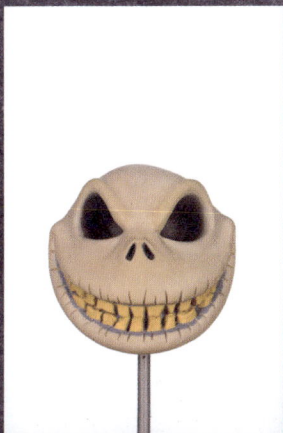

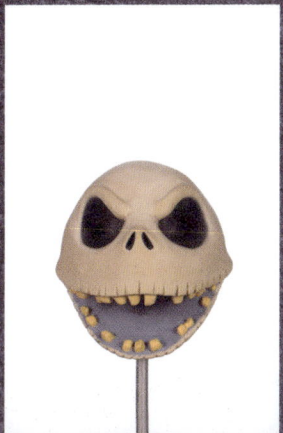

JACK (CONT'D)
(cackles maniacally)

EXT. JACK'S TOWER - DAWN

The flashes and sparks are visible through the window of Jack's
tower. Jack enters, then he steps and opens the window of his
tower. Jack looks down at some off-screen creatures.

JACK
Eureka! This year, Christmas will be ourrrrrrs!

Jack throws his arms up into the air exultantly. Sally reacts
nervously as the other creatures react with excitement.

(Overlapping, indistinct chatter and cries of joy and excitement
from the crowd)

Looking through the barred gate to Sally, who looks up sadly at
off-screen Jack.

EXT. TOWN HALL - DAY

A line of creatures file slowly toward the Town Hall.

(Overlapping, low, and indistinct chatter from the crowd)

Camera dollies in, along the line of creatures, to reveal Sally,
who waits in line.

MAYOR (OFF)
Patience, everyone. Jack has a special job for each of you.
Dr. Finkelstein!

Camera holds as Sally looks around nervously.

MAYOR (CONT'D) (OFF)
Your Christmas assignment is ready.

Sally hurries, then she kneels down and hides behind a wall. Dr.
Finkelstein enters on his wheelchair, then he stops and looks
around. Sally exits behind the wall.

MAYOR (CONT'D) (OFF)
Dr. Finkelstein, to the front of the line.

Dr. Finkelstein looks around, but does not see Sally.

DR. FINKELSTEIN
Hm.

Dr. Finkelstein drives his wheelchair and exits. Sally enters
as she pokes her head up from behind the wall.

INT. TOWN HALL - NIGHT

Vampire #1's hand, reaching in, squeezes a doll.

The doll cries.

Camera moves past Jack, sitting, to Vampire #1, who stands
center frame and holds the doll. The other three vampires
stand around him and look at the doll. Vampire #1 turns and
looks at Jack.

VAMPIRE #1
What kind of noise is that for a baby to make?

JACK
Perhaps it can be improved?

Vampire #2 and Vampire #3 gesture at Jack.

VAMPIRE #2 & VAMPIRE #3
(in unison)
No problem.

Jack waves his fist excitedly.

JACK
I knew it.

The Vampires walk and exit. Dr. Finkelstein enters through a
doorway and drives his wheelchair toward Jack.

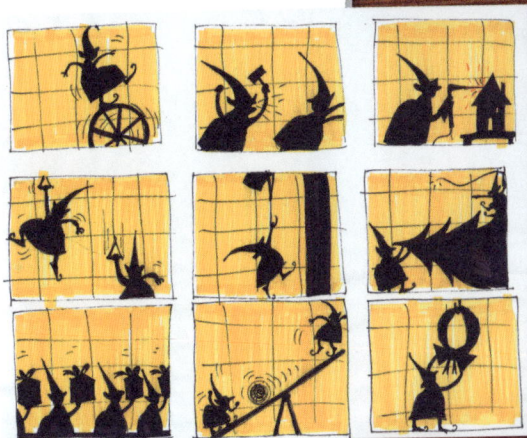

FROM PAPER TO PUPPET

Once a character design was fully approved, the drawings were handed off to sculptors, who were responsible for converting the two-dimensional illustrations into three-dimensional forms. The first step was to sculpt the character, from head to toe, in oil-based clay. "The oil-based clay is the easiest because it's very versatile and can be smoothed out with alcohol," explained Sculptor Greg Dykstra. After the sculpt was approved, a plaster mold was made so identical forms could be replicated.

To make the body, the character's custom-made steel armature was placed into the mold. Liquified foam latex was then injected to surround the armature and fill in any gaps. After the foam was cured, the body was carefully removed from the mold and taken to the fabrication department. "From that point on, the puppet belongs to my crew," Character Fabrication Supervisor Bonita DeCarlo said. After cleaning up any imperfections from the molding process, "we put on the different paint jobs, or clothing, hair, fur . . . everything else that gives the puppet its full character, and then it goes out for animation."

The movie had about sixty individual characters in all, Director Henry Selick said. "We made as many as three to four duplicates of many of those characters so the total number of puppets on this film is closer to 200."

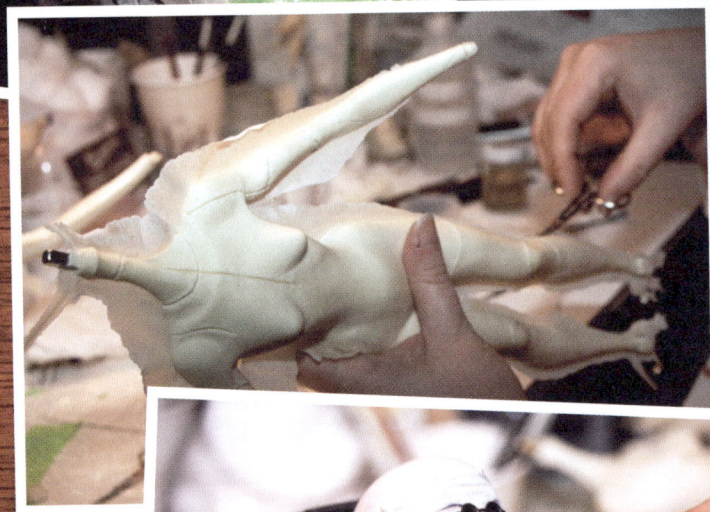

> JACK (CONT'D)
> Doctor. Thank you for coming.

Jack picks up a book.

> JACK (CONT'D)
> We need some of these.

Jack's hands hold open the book to a picture of Santa Claus, who flies across the sky with reindeer pulling his sleigh. Jack's finger points at the reindeer.

> DR. FINKELSTEIN
> Hmm. Their construction should be exceedingly simple, I think.

Low angle past Dr. Finkelstein to the Mayor, standing atop the podium with his optimistic face turned forward, and Jack.

> MAYOR
> (optimistic face)
> How horrible our Christmas will be.

Jack waves his finger at the Mayor.

> JACK
> No.

The Mayor switches to his pessimistic face.

> JACK (CONT'D)
> How jolly.

> MAYOR
> (pessimistic face)
> Oh. How jolly our Christmas will be.

A bone, a stone, and a baseball enter and hit the Mayor.

> MAYOR (CONT'D)
> (pessimistic face)
> Oo! Oh! (growls)

The Mayor turns and glares off-screen at Lock, Shock, and
Barrel.

                    MAYOR (CONT'D)
                   (pessimistic face)
        What are you doing here?

Lock, a small but insidious trick-or-treater in a devil mask,
stops and looks up at the Mayor.
                         LOCK
        Jack sent for us . . .

Shock, another insidious trick-or-treater wearing a large
witch's hat, enters, then she stops and looks up at the Mayor.

                         SHOCK
        . . . specifically . . .

Barrel, another insidious trick-or-treater wearing a skeleton
mask, enters.

                        BARREL
        . . . by name.

                         LOCK
        Lock.

                        SHOCK
        Shock.

                        BARREL
        Barrel.

The Mayor looks at Jack.

                        MAYOR
              (pessimistic face) (into megaphone)
        Jack. Jack. (without megaphone) It's (into megaphone)
        Boogie's boys.

Jack turns and looks at Lock, Shock, and Barrel.

                              JACK
          Ah.

Jack leans over, camera tilting down with him to reveal Lock,
Shock and Barrel.

                         JACK (CONT'D)
          Halloween's finest trick-or-treaters. The job I have for
               you is top secret.

Jack gestures at Lock, Shock, and Barrel.

                         JACK (CONT'D)
          It requires craft, cunning, mischief.

Lock, Shock, and Barrel look at Jack.

                              SHOCK
          And we thought you didn't like us, Jack. (chuckles)

Lock and Barrel chuckle.

Camera moves past Lock, Shock, and Barrel to Jack, who kneels
down and leans toward them.

                              JACK
          Absolutely no one is to know about it. Not a soul. Now,
          (whispering) what you must do is go to the forest.

The Mayor, standing atop the podium, holds the megaphone to
his ear and tries to listen to Jack.

                         JACK (CONT'D)
                         (whispering)
          And in the forest you will see a tree. When you get to
          the tree, open it (continues whispering indistinctly to)
          Christmas Town. Now, (continues whispering indistinctly
          to) Christmas tree and Sandy Claws and Christma tree
          (continues whispering indistinctly).

The Mayor hits the megaphone with frustration, then he reaches inside the megaphone.

                    MAYOR
               (pessimistic face)
     Ow!

The Mayor jerks his hand out of the megaphone to reveal a spider, which has bit down on his finger. The Mayor then puts the spider down on his shirt.

The spider squeaks angrily.

Camera moves past Lock, Shock, and Barrel to Jack, who kneels on the floor and leans toward them.

                    JACK
          And one more thing. Leave that no account Oogie
               Boogie out of this.

Lock starts to walk, but Jack pick him up in his hands.

                    JACK (CONT'D)
          Leave that no account . . .

Jack puts Lock down with Shock and Barrel, then he glares at them.

                    JACK (CONT'D)
          . . . Oogie Boogie out of this.

                    BARREL
          Whatever you say, Jack.

Lock, Barrel, and Shock look at Jack.

                    SHOCK
          Of course, Jack.

                    LOCK
          Wouldn't dream of it, Jack.

Lock, Shock, and Barrel chuckle.

Their hands are held behind their backs with their fingers crossed. Lock, Shock, and Barrel exit.

EXT. HALLOWEEN LAND - DAY

Lock, Shock, and Barrel walk through the town gate, then they walk down the side of a hill, camera dollying with them to reveal their treehouse, which is at the top of a gnarled, old tree. Camera dollies in toward the treehouse as Lock, Shock, and Barrel exit down into a ravine.

EXT. TREEHOUSE - DAY

Camera moves past the treehouse to Lock, Shock, and Barrel who enter from the ravine and walk toward the treehouse. They walk into an elevator cage, which is attached to ropes and used to lift people into the tree. Lock, Barrel, and Shock stand in a semicircle inside the elevator cage and stare at one another.

option #1 faces under masks are pretty much the same as the masks themselves

· BARREL · SHOCK · LOCK ·

KIDNAP THE SANDY CLAWS

Kidnap Mister Sandy Claws?

I wanna do it
Let's draw straws
Jack said we should work together
Three of a kind
Birds of a feather
Now and forever

La, la, la, la

Kidnap the Sandy Claws
Lock him up real tight
Throw away the key and then
Turn off all the lights

First we're going to set some bait
Inside a nasty trap and wait
When he comes a-sniffing we will
Snap the trap and close the gate

This concept art by Disney Studio artist Kelly Asbury uses sharp angles, twists, turns, and a moody palette for Lock, Shock, and Barrel's hideaway—the perfect setting in which to plot the kidnapping of Sandy Claws.

Wait, I've got a better plan
To catch this big red lobster man
Let's pop him in a boiling pot
And when he's done, we'll butter him up

Kidnap the Sandy Claws
Throw him in a box
Bury him for ninety years
Then see if he talks

Then Mister Oogie Boogie Man
Can take the whole thing over then
He'll be so pleased, I do declare
That he will cook him rare

Woo!

I say that we take a cannon
Aim it at his door and then
Knock three times
And when he answers
Sandy Claws will be no more

You're so stupid, think now
If we blow him up to smithereens
We may lose some pieces and then
Jack will beat us black and green

Kidnap the Sandy Claws
Tie him in a bag
Throw him in the ocean
Then see if he is sad

Because Mister Oogie Boogie
Is the meanest guy around
If I were on his boogie list
I'd get out of town

He'll be so pleased by our success
That he'll reward us, too, I bet
Perhaps he'll make his special brew
Of snake and spider stew! Mmm

We're his little henchmen and
We take our job with pride
We do our best to please him
And stay on his good side

I wish my cohorts weren't so dumb
I'm not the dumb one
You're no fun
Shut up
Make me

I've got something, listen now
This one is real good, you'll see
We'll send a present to his door
Upon there'll be a note to read

Now in the box we'll wait and hide
Until his curiosity entices him to look inside
And then we'll have him
One, two, three

Kidnap the Sandy Claws
Beat him with a stick
Lock him up for ninety years
See what makes him tick

Kidnap the Sandy Claws
Chop him into bits
Mister Oogie Boogie is sure to get his kicks

Kidnap the Sandy Claws
See what we will see
Lock him in a cage and then
Throw away the key

THE MUSIC OF NIGHTMARE

When Tim Burton wrote his original poem "The Nightmare Before Christmas," his first impulse was that the poem would make a good children's book or maybe even a holiday special for television, like the stop-motion Christmas specials he loved as a child. However, while there was some interest expressed from publishers and producers, there was not enough support to move forward at the time.

Years later, after he parted ways with Disney, and with several directorial film successes to his credit, Burton came back to his poem and his vision of bringing his story to the screen through stop-motion animation. Happily, The Walt Disney Studios was ready to take on something uniquely new yet still in the great tradition of its animation legacy. Jeffrey Katzenberg, then-chairman of Disney Studios, greenlit *Nightmare* for production, saying, "This is unlike any movie ever made before. It is a pioneering effort."

Burton had always imagined that *The Nightmare Before Christmas* would include some songs. With only his notes and sketches in hand, Burton called upon his friend and frequent collaborator—musician, singer, composer, and lyricist Danny Elfman. The two had met when Elfman was with a new wave band in the late 1970s. "I used to go see his band Oingo Boingo," Burton recalled. "They had a very animated-film-music quality to their music. [Danny] and I always kind of connected to the same thing so I knew he could do a great job."

While Burton and Elfman were laying the groundwork for developing the songs, the film's director, Henry Selick, was working out of a rundown rented soundstage in San Francisco to set up the production company that would make the film. In addition to preparing the physical space, Selick was leasing equipment, buying supplies, and hiring a production team. Selick was practically "ready to start shooting," Elfman recalled, but at this point, there was no script. "And Tim said, 'Let's start doing songs.' He would bring his drawings and lay them out on the table. It was a very organic way of developing a musical."

Elfman and Burton's collaboration on the songs expanded the story, and enthusiasm for the project grew. Elfman was surprised by how smooth and organic the process was. "I've never worked that fast," Elfman said. "But it was very simple and clear. Tim and I know each other pretty well, so there was no reason to over verbalize or over analyze."

Their method of writing songs for a musical before the script was ready was the way many musicals were written going back to the 1930s. The songs' lyrics would carry the story and would establish emotional themes, tone, and feel of the film. Burton and Elfman approached the work with no preconceived notions of what the musical style should be. As it turned out, many of the songs gravitated to an operetta style, where the songs contain segments of spoken word.

Typically, Burton would begin their sessions by telling Elfman part of the story and how the characters in the scene felt about what was happening. Burton's tale, paired with his drawings, would get Elfman's creative juices flowing.

"As we were talking, I would begin to hear music, and the instant Tim would leave, I'd begin composing the song," Elfman said. In fact, Elfman later said he felt like a kid at story time during his creative sessions with Burton. He didn't press for more information or ask about what would happen next, preferring to work only with what he'd been told. Elfman said he was

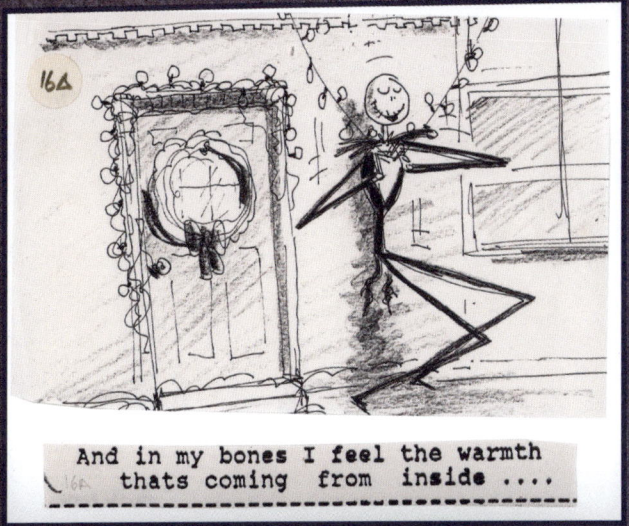

And in my bones I feel the warmth
thats coming from inside ....

Oh look, whats this?

They're hanging mistletoe ... they kiss

CAMARA PAN'S WITH JACK

Why that looks so unique ... inspired!

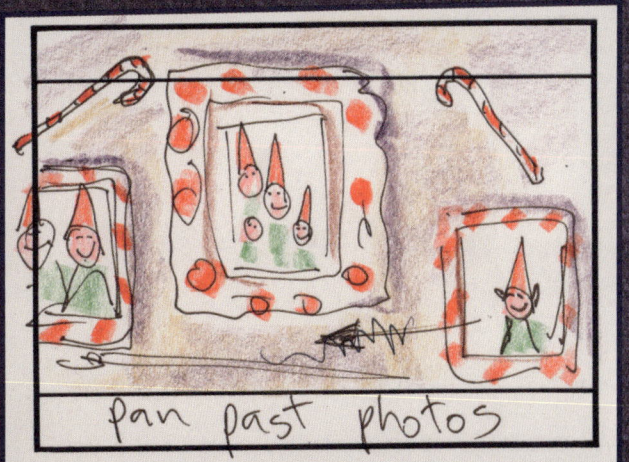

pan past photos

Theyre gathering...17B

They're gathering around to hear a story,
roasting chestnuts on a fire .... Whats this?

What's this, in here
They've got a little tree ... how queer.

And who would ever think ... and why ?
They're covering it with

often so excited to get started that he would have to ask Burton to leave. "I'd have to say, 'Please get out. I can hear the music and I have to get it down before I forget it!'"

With the completion of each song, Elfman would record it in his home studio using keyboards and musical synthesizers, and he'd sing all the parts himself. In the process of doing that, he discovered how fond he was of Jack Skellington. "I strongly related to Jack's character, and I've been through many of the same emotional beats," he said. Elfman was sure he was the best choice to be Jack's singing voice, and Burton agreed. Elfman's songs had rounded out Jack Skellington's personality and gave depth to the personalities of other characters, such as Sally, Oogie Boogie, and the tricksters Lock, Shock, and Barrel. By the time they were done, ten songs had been written, which comprised roughly half of the film's running time.

The scoring of the film had to be approached differently than other animated films. Composers commonly receive a black-and-white line drawing version of the film so they can work on the background music while the film is being finished. That was not possible with *Nightmare*. "There's either finished footage or there's no footage. There's no temporary footage," Elfman said. "As a result, I couldn't score the movie until all the animation was done."

Once he got started, the score presented Elfman with a unique challenge in that each part of the script was either leading into a song or coming out of a song. Elfman wove them together masterfully. The score became a series of musical transitions that began with a theme that related to what was just heard, then segued into a melody that introduced the song coming up. "It was like a giant jigsaw puzzle," he said. For his efforts, Elfman received numerous industry awards for his songs and score.

When Caroline Thompson came on board to write the screenplay, she created a narrative that put the songs in context and seamlessly built on the plot points and story elements in the lyrics to move the story forward. There is no major plot point in the film that isn't paired with music. The characters in the film relate to the audience, as well as each other, through song.

This looks like fun

EXT. TREEHOUSE - DAY

A walking bathtub carries Lock, Shock, and Barrel toward
the trees and into the wilderness.

INT. OOGIE BOOGIE'S DUNGEON - NIGHT

The shadow of Oogie Boogie is on the table.

                    OOGIE BOOGIE
                    (in shadow)
        Sandy Claws, huh? (laughs eerily)

A pair of dice enter and roll across the table. The dice
stops on a pair of ones. A snake enters as he slithers up
menacingly through a dot on the die.

INT. TOWN HALL - DAY

Jack, holding some sleigh bells, gestures at the skeleton
band.

                        JACK
            It goes something like this.

Jack taps out the tune to "Jingle Bells" on the sleigh bells.
Jack looks at the skeleton band.

                    JACK (CONT'D)
            How about it? Think you can manage?

The bass player holds his bass. The Man in the Bass, a man
who lives inside the bass, looks at Jack.

                    MAN IN BASS
            A-one, an' a-two, an' a-three, an' a-

Camera dollies back to reveal the accordion player and
saxophone player. The band plays a dirge-like version of
"Jingle Bells." The Mayor, at his podium, turns and looks at
the line of creatures.

                        MAYOR
                (optimistic face) (into megaphone)
            Next!

Jack gestures enthusiastically at the skeleton band. Sally
stands in line with the other creatures.

                    JACK
                 (chuckling)
          Fantastic!

The skeleton band walks.

                    JACK (CONT'D)
          Now, why don't you all practice on that and we'll be
in great shape.

Sally walks toward Jack, who turns toward her. Camera
moves past Sally to Jack, who points at her.

                    JACK (CONT'D)
          Sally. I need your help more than anyone's.

                    SALLY
          You certainly do, Jack.

Jack turns toward a toy chest.

                    SALLY (CONT'D)
          I had the most terrible vision.

Camera moves past Jack, facing and leaning over the toy
chest, to Sally, who looks anxiously at him. Jack smiles has
he searches through the chest.

                    JACK
                 (chuckling)
          That's splendid.

                    SALLY
          No! It was about your Christmas. There was smoke
          and fire and . . .

Jack shakes his head and turns toward Sally.

                    JACK
          That's not my Christmas. My Christmas is filled
with laughter and joy . . .

Jack pulls the framed drawing out of the chest, then he turns
toward Sally with it.

JACK (CONT'D)
. . . and this.

Jack holds up the framed drawing toward Sally. Jack lowers a
transparency, which shows Jack in a Santa Claus outfit, over the
framed drawing.

JACK (CONT'D)
My Sandy Claws outfit. I want you to make it.

SALLY
Jack, please listen to me. It's going to be a disaster.

JACK
How could it be?

Sally looks at Jack, who gestures at the drawing.

JACK (CONT'D)
Just follow the pattern. This part's red. The trim is white.

SALLY
It's a mistake, Jack.

JACK
Now, don't be modest. Who else is clever enough to make
my Sandy Claws outfit?

MAYOR (OFF)
(optimistic face)
Next!

Jack hands the framed drawing to Sally.

JACK
I have every confidence in you.

Sally walks and exits. Camera moves past Sally, walking, to Jack,
who steps toward the Behemoth. Sally looks up sadly.

SALLY
But it seems wrong to me. Very wrong.

Sally steps and exits. Jack reaches into the toy chest and pulls out a nutcracker, which is shaped in the form of a soldier. Jack holds the nutcracker up toward the Behemoth.

JACK
This device is called a nutcracker.

LOCK, SHOCK & BARREL (OFF)
Jack! Jack!

Jack looks at Lock, Shock, and Barrel. Lock, Shock, Barrel, and the bathtub walk up the aisle toward Jack. A sack, tied at the top, is in the bathtub.

LOCK, SHOCK & BARREL (CONT'D)
(in unison)
We caught him! We've got him!

The Behemoth holds the nutcracker and stares at it as Jack looks at Lock, Shock, and Barrel. Lock, Shock, Barrel, and the bathtub walk up the aisle toward Jack.

JACK
Perfect! Open it up. Quickly!

Jack enters and stops, then Lock, Shock, Barrel, and the bathtub stop. Lock opens the sack. The Easter Bunny pops out of the sack and exits.

Jack gasps.

The Easter Bunny reenters and lands on a seat. A banner on the Easter Bunny reads: Happy Easter. The Easter Bunny looks around with confusion. Jack looks at the Easter Bunny with shock. Jack turns and looks at Lock, Shock, and Barrel.

JACK (CONT'D)
That's not Sandy Claws.

THE CUTTING ROOM FLOOR

Before computerized editing systems came along, movies were edited by hand, which involved physically cutting processed film between frames to remove or insert a shot and then splicing the film back together with adhesive or tape. As a result, an editor's "cutting room floor" would typically be littered with pieces of movie film that were shots and scenes that had been literally cut from the film. There were many reasons why material would be removed, such as technical problems, multiple takes, or actors flubbing their lines. These outtakes, especially the ones showing an actor's mistakes, have often been cut into amusing mini programs of their own.

By contrast, there are precious few outtakes on a stop-motion movie. However, one such example from *Tim Burton's The Nightmare Before Christmas* comes late in the film, as the townspeople of Halloween Town are playing in the snow. The scene in question shows the three vampires playing hockey on the pond, using a pumpkin head as a puck. But in the original shot, which ended up, figuratively, on the cutting room floor, the vampires were actually using an image of Tim Burton's head as the puck! But by and large, the painstaking, time-consuming, and costly process of shooting a film frame by frame means that many of the critical decisions a director needs to make are decided in the storyboarding stage, long before anything is shot.

"In live action they shoot coverage," said Storyboard Supervisor Joe Ranft, referring to the practice of shooting multiple takes of every scene. "In animation you don't have that luxury. In storyboarding, you can at least try different versions of things."

The final storyboards are broken down into discreet scenes, which the animators use to rehearse and do a series of short test shots. Once everything is worked out, the goal is to have the scenes that go before the camera for their "hero" take be the final take that will appear in the finished film.

In *Tim Burton's The Nightmare Before Christmas*, some of the segments that were cut at the storyboarding stage survived. Perhaps the most surprising one is an alternate ending that was considered early on but rejected. It begins with Oogie Boogie standing atop the eightball in his dungeon as he attempts to escape from Jack. As seen in the final film, Oogie Boogie's outfit splits at the seams and creepy-crawly things tumble out. But in this version, when Oogie Boogie's outfit splits, it's revealed that Dr. Finkelstein is inside! The mad scientist, who created Sally, was jealous of her love for Jack and wanted to teach her a lesson "that she'd never forget!" The boards go on to show a trap door in the roulette wheel opening and Igor snatching Dr. Finkelstein away with a giant claw. The scene ends with Jack looking into the camera and saying, "I don't believe this."

While this turn of events was surprising and humorous, it would have changed the trajectory of the story significantly. Having the villain escape would have set up an expectation for the audience of him one day returning in a sequel, which would have been a lingering loose end that would take away from Burton's vision of Jack and Sally's emotional happily-ever-after ending.

RRRRip!

24C rev

NE 5

EVIL SCIENTIST(O.S.):

You've crossed the line this time, Jack!

NE 2

OOGIE/EVIL SCIENTIST:
Now you've done it, Jack...

NE 28

EVIL SCIENTIST:
Farewell - Jack Skellington !

SHOCK

It isn't?

BARREL

Who is it?

The Easter Bunny enters and hops down the aisle toward the
Behemoth. The Easter Bunny stops and stares at the Behemoth.
The Easter Bunny sniffs the Behemoth.

The Easter Bunny sniffs.

The Behemoth points at the Easter Bunny.

BEHEMOTH

Bunny!

The Easter Bunny recoils in fear. Lock, Shock, and Barrel and
Jack look down at the bathtub. The Easter Bunny enters and
immediately exits back into the sack.

The Easter Bunny whimpers.

Jack turns and looks at Lock, Shock, and Barrel with
exasperation. Jack gestures at Lock, Shock, and Barrel.

JACK

Not Sandy Claws. Take him back.

Lock, Shock, and Barrel look at Jack.

LOCK

We followed your instructions.

BARREL

We went through the door.

Camera moves past Lock, Shock, and Barrel to Jack, who gestures
at them with exasperation.

JACK

Which door? There's more than one. Sandy Claws is
behind the door shaped like . . .

Jack pulls a cookie, which is shaped like a Christmas tree, out of his pocket.

                         JACK (CONT'D)
         . . . this.

Jack's hand enters as he holds up the cookie. Lock, Shock, and Barrel look accusingly at one another.

                         SHOCK
         I told you.

Shock starts to strangle Lock.

Lock grunts.

Barrel punches at Shock, but misses her.

Barrel grunts.

Barrel falls to the floor, then Lock knocks Shock down to the floor. Jack, looking at Lock, Shock, and Barrel, rubs his head with exasperation.

                         LOCK
                      (grunts)
         Knock it off!

Shock grunts and yelps in pain.

Jack pulls at the corners of his mouth and makes a scary face.

Jack roars.

Barrel, Shock, and Lock gape at Jack. Lock, Shock, and Barrel gasp.

Jack leans toward the sack, which contains the Easter Bunny. The bag shakes as the Easter Bunny trembles with fear.

                         JACK
         I'm very sorry for the inconvenience, sir.

The Easter Bunny whimpers.

Jack turns and glares at Lock, Shock, and Barrel.

                    JACK (CONT'D)
          Take him home first. And apologize again!

The bathtub walks and exits. Camera moves past Jack to the bathtub,
which walks toward the door. Lock, Shock, and Barrel enter as they
follow the bathtub.

                    JACK (CONT'D)
          Be careful with Sandy Claws when you fetch him! Treat him
          nicely!

                         LOCK
          Got it!

                         SHOCK
          We'll get it right . . .

                    LOCK, SHOCK & BARREL
                         (in unison)
          . . . next time!

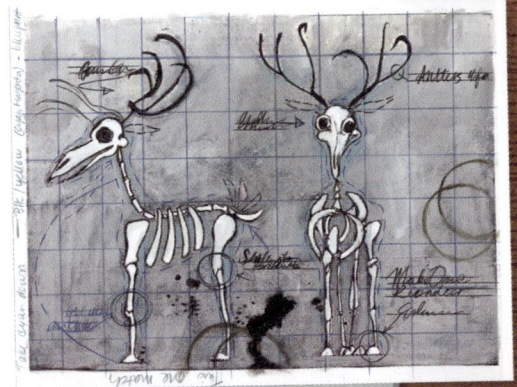

Lock, Shock, Barrel, and the bathtub walk through the doorway, then
the doors close and obscure them.

INT. DR. FINKELSTEIN'S HOUSE/LABORATORY - DAY

Dr. Finkelstein, sitting in his wheelchair, looks at a female body,
which is strapped to a bench. A machine makes measurements for a
head.

                    DR. FINKELSTEIN
          You will be a decided improvement over that treacherous
          Sally.

                    IGOR (OFF)
          Master!

Dr. Finkelstein turns and looks at Igor. Igor, a one-eyed
hunchbacked creature, carries some rolled-up plans toward a table.

                    IGOR (CONT'D)
          The plans.

Igor unrolls the plans on the table. Dr. Finkelstein enters, then drives his wheelchair to a stop in front of the table.

DR. FINKELSTEIN

Excellent, Igor.

Dr. Finkelstein lifts a box of dog bones into frame. Dr. Finkelstein tosses a dog bone, then Igor catches the bone in his mouth. Igor chews the food as Dr. Finkelstein studies the plans.

EXT. TOWN HALL - DAY

A clock is on the top of the Town Hall. A sign, below the clock, reads: "036 Days to Halloween." The sign changes to read: "035 Days to Xmas." Camera cranes down, off the clock, and moves back across the square to reveal creatures, who move in all directions as they make preparations for Christmas. The Devil holds up some sleigh bells.

DEVIL

Ah.

The Harlequin Demon opens a box.

Harlequin Demon growls.

The Wolfman puts down a table.

Wolfman growls.

Camera moves off the creatures to reveal Sally, who sits at a sewing machine and works on the Santa Claus outfit.

· DEVIL ·

TOP VIEW / FULL SCALE

MAKING CHRISTMAS

This time, this time

Making Christmas
Making Christmas
Making Christmas
Making Christmas
Is so fine

It's ours this time
And won't the children be surprised
It's ours this time

Making Christmas
Making Christmas
Making Christmas

Time to give them something fun
They'll talk about for years to come
Let's have a cheer from everyone
It's time to party

Making Christmas
Making Christmas
Making Christmas
Making Christmas
Making Christmas

Sticks and mice get wrapped up so nice
With spider legs and pretty bows
It's ours this time

All together, that and this
With all our tricks
We're making Christmastime

Here comes Jack.

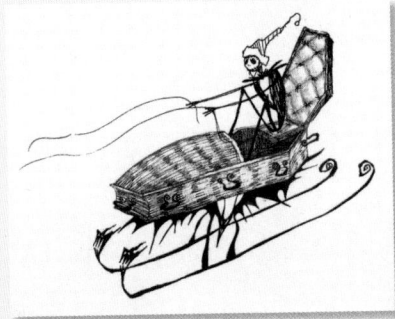

I don't believe what's happening to me
My hopes, my dreams, my fantasies

Won't they be impressed, I am a genius
See how I transformed this old rat
Into a most delightful hat

My compliments from me to you
On this your most intriguing hat
Consider though this substitute
A bat in place of this old rat

No, no, no, now that's all wrong

This thing will never make a present

It's been dead for much too long

Try something fresher, something pleasant

Try again, don't give up

All together, that and this

With all our tricks

We're making Christmastime

Camera tilts up to reveal the clock on the Town Hall. The sign reads: "035 Days to Xmas." Camera moves in as the sign changes to read: "034 Days to Xmas." The sign changes to read: "033 Days to Xmas." The sign changes to read: "032 Days to Xmas."

EXT. CHRISTMAS TOWN STREETS - NIGHT

The hands on a clock, which is on a chimney, spin. A sign above the clock reads: Christmas Town. The hands on the clock stop spinning and point at lettering that reads: "Dec 25." Sign below clock reads: "Days Left 012." A sign below the clock changes to read: "Days Left 011."

INT. CHRISTMAS TOWN FACTORY - NIGHT

Elves supervise an assembly line, which manufactures rocking horses. Elves sew teddy bear patterns onto doilies.

INT. CHRISTMAS TOWN BAKERY - DAY

An elf carries some wood toward a furnace. Some gingerbread men roll on a conveyer belt. Camera moves in as the elf opens the furnace. Camera continues to move in, off the elf, on the wood, which burns in the furnace.

Scene wipes right to left in a clock-shaped pattern.

INT. DR. FINKELSTEIN'S HOUSE/LABORATORY - NIGHT

Igor's hands hold a lamp. Camera moves back slightly to reveal
Igor and Dr. Finkelstein, who sits in his wheelchair. Dr.
Finkelstein pulls on a lever.

Dr. Finkelstein sits and Igor stands. Some reindeer skeletons
are lying on a table. Huge electrodes shoot electricity into the
reindeer skeletons. The reindeer skeletons float up into the air.

Dr. Finkelstein and Igor look up at the reindeer skeletons, which
float up into the air. Camera moves in, off Igor and the reindeer
skeletons, on Dr. Finkelstein, who flops down on the table. Camera
tilts down to reveal the table and a skeleton head, which is on it.
Dr. Finkelstein picks up the skeleton head and begins to clean it.

Scene wipes right to left in a clock-shaped pattern.

INT. CHRISTMAS TOWN FACTORY - DAY

An elf rubs down the side of Santa's sleigh. Camera moves back to
reveal more elves, who are cleaning Santa's sleigh. Camera holds as
reindeer enter and cross.

An elf pushes a Jack-in-the-box head down into its box.

INT. EVIL JACK-IN-THE-BOX - DAY

Looking up out of the Jack-in-the-box at the elf, who peers down
into it. The elf closes the Jack-in-the-box's lid, obscuring himself.

The lid of the box opens to reveal the clown. The clown puts a
Jack-o'-lantern down inside the box, then he starts to close the
lid.

EXT. HALLOWEEN TOWN SQUARE - DAY

Looking over a table, with several evil Jack-in-the-boxes on it, to
the Clown, who looks at them.

INT. CHRISTMAS TOWN FACTORY - DAY

An elf uses a machine to fill up
stockings, which roll past him
on a conveyor belt.

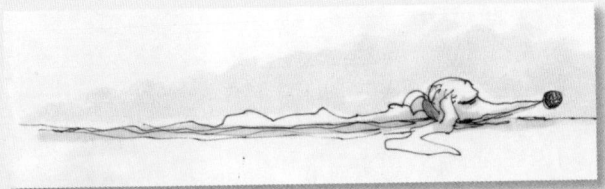

EXT. HALLOWEEN TOWN - DAY

A snake is to the right as the saxophone player looks through some
skulls. The saxophone player puts a skull into the mouth of the
snake, but the snake bites down on the saxophone player.

INT. CHRISTMAS TOWN FACTORY - DAY

An elf uses a crane to lift a box of toys into the air. The crane
swings the bag of toys.

Scene wipes right to left in a clock-shaped pattern.

EXT. HALLOWEEN TOWN SQUARE - NIGHT
Jack stands and faces toward a pulley, which lowers a coffin toward
him.

MAKING CHRISTMAS

(Part 2)

This time, this time, this time, this time
Making Christmas
Making Christmas
La la la

It's almost here and we can't wait
So ring the bells and celebrate
'Cause when the full moon starts to climb
We'll all sing out
"It's Christmastime!"

JACK AND SALLY

Despite its sometimes macabre nature, *Tim Burton's The Nightmare Before Christmas* is a positive story, with characters who are trying to do a good thing but get a bit "mixed up" in the process. Capturing their inner feelings and emotional responses in the film was creatively achieved through the physical designs of the puppets, their costumes, and, of course, the animation.

Jack is a multi-faceted protagonist with a wide range of emotions and feelings. He exudes confidence and leadership; feels sadness, melancholy, joy, and confusion; and ultimately expresses self-awareness and love. To the citizens of Halloween Town, he seems to have it all, but he is, in fact, discontent. "His melancholy comes from his loneliness and isolation, from his feelings of '"been there, done that,'" Screenwriter Caroline Thompson said.

On the exterior, Jack has a regal bearing; he's tall, slender, and moves with an elegant, almost spider-like precision. Jack's dapper manner is reminiscent of a legendary actor and dancer, according to Tim Burton. "I was just sort of thinking of people like Fred Astaire," he said. "[Jack] was thin but it gave him an elegance, and . . . a certain theatricality."

"There's a very definite style to the way Jack walks," Animator Paul Berry said. "It defines what his whole personality is about." Berry was mindful of how Jack's inner emotions impacted the way he moved. "When you animate Jack from the outside, you have to deal with what's inside him as well," he said.

Jack's creator finds both beauty and sadness in the way Jack is misperceived by others. "Thematically that's something that I like, still respond to, and have responded to in other films about that type of character, somebody like the Grinch, who is perceived as scary but isn't," Burton said.

Like Jack, Sally dreams of something more than the life she's been given. No one would ever describe Sally as elegant. She is, in fact, a Frankenstein-esque rag doll, with stitched-together body parts and a dress made from various pieces of scrap material. She walks with a wobble and is not a conventional beauty, though in Halloween Town nobody thinks twice about her looks.

Thompson had issues with the way Sally was originally portrayed. Burton's early drawings depicted her as being sassy and curvaceous, not at all what Thompson had in mind. Her inclination was to make Sally a sort of "Little Match Girl": sweet, innocent, tragic. The resolution came when Sally was redesigned as an unpretentious, waifish young woman. When Thompson viewed early test footage and saw the determined but slightly off-balanced way Sally moved, she knew the character needed to have the same determination built into her persona.

Burton says the character of Sally came from somewhere deep within him. "She came out of drawings with this strange stitching image that I'd been thinking about for a while," Burton said. "The feeling of not being together . . . and of constantly trying to pull yourself together, so to speak."

The beauty of Sally is that while she often, literally, goes to pieces, she knows herself and understands what she needs to be emotionally whole. When Jack finally realizes how much she loves him and acknowledges his own feelings toward her, their embrace at the top of Spiral Hill has all the emotional punch of a classic Hollywood ending.

Sheet 1 (top)

SHOT BREAKDOWN   **Updated 12/4/92**

| Set Up 7/31/92 | Light 3 | Prep 2 | Shoot 4 | Date Seq. Sched to begin 12/18/92 | Shot# 1400/15 | Sketch # 7A-7B |

Song Jack & Sally Duet

Location Cemetery
Time of day Night or dawn (TBD)

Description
WS - Jack walks up to the top of the hill with his arms outstretched towards Sally. They are singing.

as anyone   can see

Characters Needed
Jack, Sally

Character Notes

Sculpted/Fabricated Props

Model Props

Dialogue: Jack and Sally: "...as anyone can see.."
Approved [X]

Rigs

Camera
Possible off center push in. Safeguard camera move data for easy duplication on stars, and snow elements. Give Pete fully documented camera move data for later snow matching.

Opticals
Undetermined FX Animation - Falling snow

Cel Animation
Undetermined FX Animation - Falling snow

Notes

Stage Set# CEM*5
Spiral Hill

Lights
Practical moon if move permits
Pumpkins in the BG should be prepared to light up

Dissolves/Fades
None

Redressed with snow and winter FX; icicles, fiber optic glints, etc. Crunchable snow for footprints only where Sally & Jack

*Dates & frames WILL CHANGE. Check the big

Sheet 2 (right)

SHOT BREAKDOWN   **Updated 4/20/93**

| Set Up 8/30/92 | Light 3 | Prep 2 | Shoot 5 | Date Seq. Sched to begin 12/18/92 | Shot# 1400/11 | Sketch # 9A-9H |

Song Jack & Sally Duet

Location Cemetery
Time of day Night

Description
WS - Jack and Sally embrace and kiss on Spiral Hill. Zero enters into frame and flies across frame to other side of Spiral Hill. TILT UP with Zero as he flies in a circle and disappears into a starburst.

Characters Needed
Jack, Sally, Zero

Character Notes
Happy dog

Sculpted/Fabricated Props

Model Props

Dialogue: None
Approved [X]

Rigs

Camera
Tilt. Safeguard camera move data for easy duplication on stars, snow, Zero elements. Give Pete fully documented camera move data for later snow matching.

Opticals
Zero composite

Cel Animation
None

Notes

Stage Set# CEM*5
Spiral Hill

Redressed with snow and winter FX; icicles, fiber optic glints, etc. Crunchable snow for footprints only where Sally & Jack walk. Hard snow where animators need to work.

Frame Count: 387
Seconds: 16.13

and check with Editorial for accurate frame counts.

Sheet 3 (bottom)

SHOT BREAKDOWN   **Updated 12/4/92**

| Set Up 7/31/92 | Light 2 | Prep 2 | Shoot 3 | Date Seq. Sched to begin 12/18/92 | Shot# 1400/16 | Sketch # 8,8B |

Song Jack & Sally Duet

Location Cemetery
Time of day Night or dawn (TBD)

Description
CU - Jack and Sally face each other as they continue to sing. Slow PUSH IN as the song ends.

we're surely meant to be

Characters Needed
Jack, Sally

Character Notes

Sculpted/Fabricated Props

Model Props

Dialogue: Jack and Sally: "...we're surely meant to be."
Approved [X]

Rigs

Camera
Romantic push in. Safeguard camera move data for easy duplication on stars, and snow elements. Give Pete fully documented camera move data for later snow matching.
Same as 1400/12

Opticals
Undetermined FX Animation - Falling snow

Cel Animation
Undetermined FX Animation - Falling snow

Notes

Stage Set# CEM*5
Spiral Hill

Lights
Practical moon

Dissolves/Fades
None

Redressed with snow and winter FX; icicles, fiber optic glints, etc. Crunchable snow for footprints only where Sally & Jack walk. Hard snow where animators need to work.

Frame Count: 167
Seconds: 6.96

*Dates & frames WILL CHANGE. Check the big board for accurate dates and check with Editorial for accurate frame counts.

EXT. HALLOWEEN TOWN SQUARE - NIGHT

Camera moves in on the clock, the sign below which reads: "002 Days to Xmas." The sign changes to read: "001 Days to Xmas."

INT. SANTA CLAUS'S COTTAGE - DAY

Mrs. Claus faces into kitchen.

> SANTA CLAUS (OFF)
> Kathleen . . . Bobby . . . Susie.

The face of Mrs. Claus enters as she turns and slides a pie into the oven.

> SANTA CLAUS (OFF) (CONT'D)
> Yes, Susie's been nice. Nice . . . nice . . .

Camera moves back, off Mrs. Claus, to reveal Santa Claus, who reads from a long list.

> SANTA CLAUS (CONT'D)
> . . . naughty . . . nice . . . nice . . . nice. There are hardly any naughty children this year.

Camera tilts up to reveal the face of Santa Claus. The doorbell rings.

> SANTA CLAUS (CONT'D)
> Now, who could that be?

EXT. SANTA CLAUS'S COTTAGE - DAY

Lock, Barrel, and Shock look at the front door of the cottage. The door opens to reveal Santa Claus.

> LOCK, SHOCK & BARREL
> (in unison)
> Trick or treat!

Santa Claus looks down at Lock, Shock, and Barrel with surprise.

> SANTA CLAUS
> Huh?

> LOCK, SHOCK & BARREL

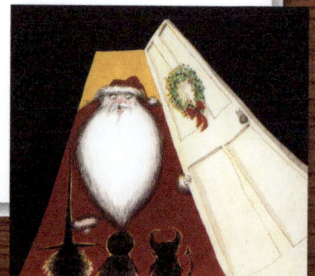

Eeee-yah!

Lock, Shock, and Barrel leap forward with a sack, which fills
the frame.

EXT. HALLOWEEN TOWN SQUARE - DAY

Camera moves past Sally, tipping in and out, to a mirror, which
shows a reflection of Jack, who stands still as Sally sews
alterations onto his Santa Claus costume. Jack also wears a
fake Santa Claus beard.

                    SALLY
          You don't look like yourself, Jack. Not at all.

                    JACK
          Isn't that wonderful?

Camera dollies back to fully reveal Sally and to reveal Jack,
who stands and looks at his reflection in the mirror.

                    JACK (CONT'D)
          It couldn't be more wonderful.

Sally takes the framed photograph off the wall, then she holds
it up toward Jack.

                    SALLY
          But you're the Pumpkin King.

Sally lifts the transparency of Jack as Santa Claus to reveal
the drawing of Jack as the Pumpkin King.

                    JACK
          Not anymore.

Jack enters and takes the framed drawing from Sally. Jack
cracks the framed drawing over his knee.

                    JACK (CONT'D)
          And I feel so much better now.

Camera moves past Jack's arm, reaching in, to Sally, who looks
down sadly at it. Sally starts to sew on the sleeve of the
Santa Claus outfit.

SALLY
Jack, I know you think something's missing, but . . .

Sally accidently pokes Jack in the finger with her needle.

JACK
Ow!

SALLY
Sorry.

Jack kisses his finger. Jack gestures at Sally.

JACK
You're right. Something is missing.

Sally smiles hopefully. Jack leans and stares at his reflection in the mirror. The mirror shows an out-of-focus reflection of Lock, Shock, Barrel, and the bathtub.

JACK (CONT'D)
But what? I've got the beard, the coat, the boots, the belt . . .

LOCK, SHOCK & BARREL (in mirror)
(in unison)
Jack! Jack!

Jack turns and looks at Lock, Shock, and Barrel. Camera moves focus, off Jack, to the reflection of Lock, Shock, Barrel, and the bathtub in the mirror.

LOCK, SHOCK & BARREL (CONT'D)
(in unison)
This time we bagged him.

Lock, Shock, and Barrel lead the bathtub, which holds the sack with Santa Claus inside it, across the square. Creatures stand in all parts of the square. Jack enters and walks toward them.

LOCK
This time we really did.

Shock and Lock stand on either side of the bathtub and look at Jack. Barrel enters as he hangs down from the top of the sack in the bathtub.

                          BARREL
          He sure is big, Jack.

                          SHOCK
          And heavy.

                    SANTA CLAUS (OFF)
            Let . . .

Lock and Shock pull on the strings of the sack, then Santa Claus pops out of the sack.

                    SANTA CLAUS (CONT'D)
            . . . me out!

Santa Claus's cap is jerked down over his eyes. The creatures look at Santa Claus and react with shock.

The crowd gasps.

Jack's hand, reaching in, shakes Santa Claus's hand, which reaches in. Santa Claus hangs out of the top of the sack. Jack enters, then he stops and gestures at Santa Claus.

                          JACK
          Sandy Claws. In person.

Jack shakes hands with Santa Claus.

                       JACK (CONT'D)
          What a pleasure to meet you.

Santa Claus hangs out of the top of the sack as Jack stares down at his hands.

                       JACK (CONT'D)
          Why, you have hands. You don't have claws at all.

Santa Claus pulls the cap off his eyes, then he looks at the creatures with surprise. From Santa's point of view, out of focus image as camera moves across the creatures to reveal Jack, who looks at Santa Claus.

(Overlapping, low, and indistinct chatter continues under
following scenes and dialogue)

The Wolfman growls.

                        SANTA CLAUS
        Wh-Wh-Where am I?

                        JACK
        Surprised, aren't you? I knew you would be. You don't need to
        have another worry about Christmas this year.

Camera dollies off Jack's face to reveal some creatures, who
hold up toys. Santa Claus, hanging out of the sack, gapes at the
creatures.

                        SANTA CLAUS
        What? Wh-what? Wh-

Jack enters, then he crouches down and gestures at Santa Claus.
Santa Claus looks down at a rat. A rat, nibbling on some cheese,
looks up at Santa Claus. The rat squeaks.

                        JACK
        Consider this a vacation, Sandy. A reward. It's your turn to
        take it easy.

Santa Claus gestures at Jack with disbelief.

                        SANTA CLAUS
        B-but there must be some mistake.

Shock enters and Lock enters, then Jack looks at them.

                        JACK
        See that he's comfortable.

Jack peers thoughtfully at Santa Claus.

                        JACK (CONT'D)
        Just a second, fellas. Of course! That's what I'm missing.

Jack takes the cap off of Santa Claus's head and puts it on his
own head.

                         SANTA CLAUS
          B-b-but . . .

                            JACK
          Thanks.

Jack walks and exits as Santa Claus gestures frantically
at him.

                         SANTA CLAUS
          You just can't . . .

Lock and Shock pull the drawstrings on the bag, closing it
and obscuring Santa Claus.

                     SANTA CLAUS (CONT'D)
                       (through bag)
          Hold on!

The bathtub carries Santa Claus.

                     SANTA CLAUS (CONT'D)
                       (through bag)
          Where are we going now?

Jack practices being Santa Claus.

                            JACK
          Ho, ho, ho.

Jack shakes his head.

                        JACK (CONT'D)
          No.

Sally looks sadly at Jack. A mirror shows a reflection of
Jack as he practices being Santa Claus.

                           SALLY
          This is worse than I thought. Much worse.

                            JACK
                        (in mirror)
          Oh, ho, ho.

FLIRTING WITH DISASTER

One of the key differences between cel animation and stop-motion animation is that if an error is made on a frame or two in cel animation, that art can be repaired or redone and edited into the sequence. But stop-motion animation is different and, in a way, closer to what happens in a live-action production. If there's an error, those frames cannot be recreated and cut into the film. It's virtually impossible to match the exact motion, lighting conditions, and camera positions, which means the entire sequence has to be reshot. On a live-action film, the retake happens in real time. But in stop-action, the retake is done one frame at a time. Supervising Animator Eric Leighton gave the example of a 400-frame shot, which, at twenty-four frames per second is about seventeen seconds of movie but would take about ten days to shoot. The time and expense of reshoots was a considerable strain on the budget and schedule.

Early on, Storyboard Supervisor Joe Ranft came to realize how precise his drawings needed to be. "At the beginning, I didn't even know what the problems were. Set guys would come up to me and say, 'See what your little drawings made us do?' They . . . had to build ten more feet on a set because of the angle I chose!" In 2-D animation, a background artist would just paint that in. But with stop-motion, a full set extension had to be constructed.

Keeping the number of reshoots to a minimum was a priority for Producer Kathleen Gavin, but there were always unexpected challenges. Gavin recalled one particularly nettlesome challenge that came early in the production. Each set for the film had a full array of up to twenty or thirty lighting instruments, and sometimes during filming, a single bulb would burn out and not be noticed. But when the completed scene was screened in dailies, the brightness shift would be noticeable, and the entire scene would have to be reshot. There didn't seem to be a way to contain the problem until a technician devised a "black box" that measured the total voltage going into the lighting equipment. If a bulb went out, the voltage would drop and a warning light would click on, giving the gaffers the opportunity to find and replace the bulb and save the scene.

One of Associate Producer Phil Lofaro's favorite disaster stories occurred when the film crew was moving a large motion control boom arm from one side of a stage to the other while an animator was working on a shot with Oogie Boogie. The boom knocked the camera's dolly track out of position by a foot. The animator, who'd been working on the shot for two weeks, was inconsolable. While Lofaro and the crew were trying to figure out what to do, Pete Kozachik, the director of photography, grabbed a two-by-four and levered the track back in place by lining it up to the dust marks on the floor. "There," Kozachik said. "Now, keep shooting."

Those examples were typical of the can-do attitude that contributed to the genuine esprit de corps that flourished among the staff and crew. The *Tim Burton's The Nightmare Before Christmas* project was so unique—and the opportunity to create a feature-length stop-motion film so rare—that all involved wanted to see the project succeed, no matter what challenges came along. "Everybody was so passionate about the project," Lofaro said. "Everyone loved the work and were grateful to be able to do it."

Sally looks up hopefully.

                    SALLY
     I know!

                    JACK
                 (in mirror)
          Ho, ho . . . ho?

Sally turns and walks.

EXT. HALLOWEEN LAND - DAY

Lock and Shock accompany the bathtub, which
carries Barrel and the sack, through the main gate.

                    SANTA CLAUS
                 (through bag)
          Me on vacation? On Christmas Eve?

                    BARREL
          Where are we taking him?

                    SHOCK
     Where?

The group stops, then Lock looks at Shock and Barrel.

                    LOCK
          To Oogie Boogie, of course. There isn't anywhere
          in the whole world more comfortable than that.
          And Jack said to make him comfortable, didn't he?

Shock and Barrel nod their heads.

                    SHOCK & BARREL
                 (in unison)
          Yes, he did.

                    SANTA CLAUS
                 (through bag)
          Haven't you heard of peace on Earth and
          goodwill toward men?

Lock, Shock, and Barrel shake their heads at the sack.

                    LOCK, SHOCK & BARREL
                       (in unison)
                 No! (overlapping giggles)

Camera tilts up as Lock, Shock, Barrel, and the bathtub exit.

INT. DR. FINKELSTEIN'S HOUSE/SALLY'S ROOM - DUSK

Sally, kneeling on the floor, has removed a floor plank and
reaches down under the floor.

Sally grunts. Sally pulls a jug out from the floor. Sally's
hands, reaching in, hold a jug. The lettering on the jug reads:
Fog Juice.

                         SALLY
          This will stop Jack.

Sally replaces the floor plank in the floor.

Sally hears the sound of Dr. Finkelstein's machines. Sally
stands up and walks toward the door.

INT. DR. FINKELSTEIN'S HOUSE/CORRIDOR - DUSK

Some valves spin on Dr. Finkelstein's equipment. Sally enters
and walks, camera moving with her to reveal the laboratory
doorway, through which Dr. Finkelstein is visible as he sits
in his chair and works on his new creation. Camera holds as
Sally stops and peers at Dr. Finkelstein.

INT. DR. FINKELSTEIN'S HOUSE/LABORATORY - DUSK

Dr. Finkelstein, sitting, looks at his creation, which is in a
chair. The creation, which is still wrapped in bandages, is
shaped to look like Dr. Finkelstein. Sally is visible through
the corridor doorway.

                    DR. FINKELSTEIN
          What a joy to think of all we'll have in common.

Dr. Finkelstein opens the top of his creation's head, then he
opens his own head.

DR. FINKELSTEIN (CONT'D)
We'll have conversations worth having.

Dr. Finkelstein pulls half of his brain out of his head, then he drops his brain into his creation's head. Dr. Finkelstein kisses the brain. Sally hurries down the corridor and exits.

EXT. TREEHOUSE - NIGHT

The lights are on in the treehouse.

LOCK, SHOCK & BARREL (OFF)
(mischievous giggles)

INT. TREEHOUSE - NIGHT

Camera looks through the pipe and past Lock and Shock, standing, to the bathtub, which carries the sack, with Santa Claus hanging out the front of it. Barrel sits on top of the sack.

SANTA CLAUS
Don't do this! Naughty children never get any presents.

LOCK, SHOCK & BARREL
(overlapping, mischievous giggles)

The bathtub shoves Santa Claus into the pipe, obscuring Lock, Shock, and Barrel. Lock, Shock, and Barrel try to push Santa Claus, who is stuck in the mouth of the mask, into the pipe.

SHOCK
I think he might be too big.

Santa Claus is forced further down the pipe. Santa Claus groans.

LOCK
No, he's not.

Lock, Shock, and Barrel push harder on Santa Claus.

If he can go down a chimney, he can fit down here.

Santa Claus groans. Santa Claus exits as he slides down the pipe.

EXT. TREEHOUSE - NIGHT

Camera tilts down along the pipe as Santa Claus squeezes down through it.

INT. OOGIE BOOGIE'S DUNGEON - NIGHT

The bottom of the pipe extends down from the ceiling. Santa Claus enters as he drops out of the pipe, camera tilting down with him as he lands
on the table. Camera moves in as Santa Claus turns and stares at an off-screen throne.

Camera moves in on Oogie Boogie's throne. The throne is outlined with spooky white light.

Camera dollies in on some bats, who hang down from the ceiling. The bats are outlined in spooky white light. The bats squeak.

Camera moves in on Santa Claus, who lies on the table with his hands tied.

Some towers, made of dice, stand on either side of a gate. The gate opens, then a pair of dice enter and roll across the floor.

Santa Claus lies on the table. The dice enter, then they roll to a stop on the table. A huge shadow crosses Santa Claus, then he turns and looks up at Oogie Boogie.

Oogie Boogie, a huge, malevolent creature, made out of a sack which is filled with bugs, snakes, and creepie-crawlies, looks down at Santa Claus.

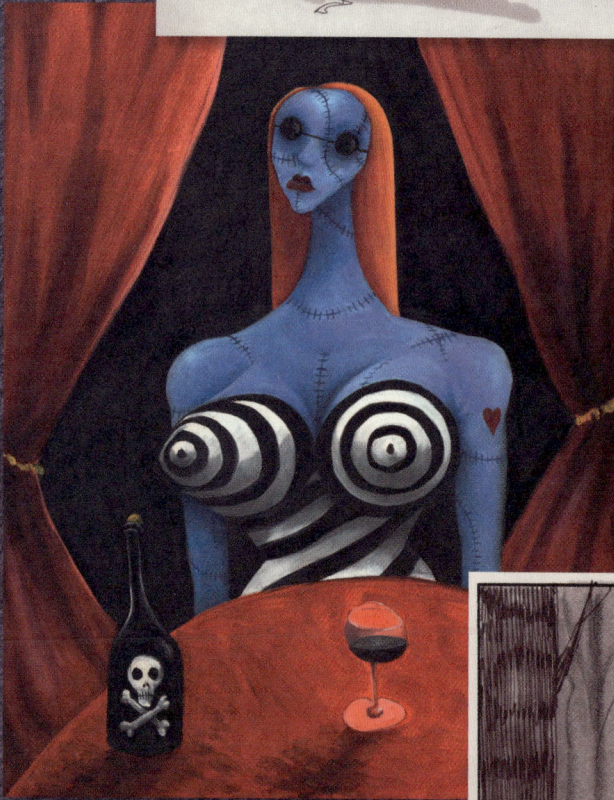

A CELEBRATION OF THE ART OF BURTON

On November 22, 2009, an exhibition of Tim Burton's artistic life opened at the Museum of Modern Art (MoMA) in New York City. It contained hundreds of pieces of his work that ranged from early childhood drawings through his later work in film and sculpture. The catalogue accompanying the exhibit, written by MoMA staff, heralded the impact of Burton's work: "Taking inspiration from popular culture, Tim Burton has reinvented Hollywood genre filmmaking as an expression of personal vision, garnering for himself an international audience of fans and influencing a generation of young artists working in film, video, and graphics."

MoMA has always considered filmmakers to be artists, no matter that making a film is a very collaborative effort. For the Tim Burton exhibit, the script would be flipped, with his films taking a backseat to a significant collection of his work in 2-D and 3-D mediums.

For the curators of the exhibit, the challenge was to interpret Burton's unique and restless creative imagination for an art museum audience. They searched for pieces in movie studio archives, small independent production companies, the homes of private collectors, and Burton's private collection, which they estimated contained about 10,000 items. Burton had essentially been his own archivist starting from a young age. His files were full of pop-culture-based elements, from sketches, drawings, and doodles to newspaper and magazine clippings, outlines, unfinished writing projects, and much, much more. By early 2009, the curators had identified more than 500 pieces they wanted to display. Burton recommended adding another forty to the list.

Burton was enthusiastic about the project. "So, all these years later, to have this exhibition, to be showing things—some of which weren't meant to ever be seen or are just pieces of the larger picture—is very special to me," Burton said.

To make the exhibit as current as possible, Burton created seven new sculptural pieces, including a six-foot-tall rotating, fluorescent carousel accompanied by music by Danny Elfman, and a twenty-two-foot tall inflatable called Balloon Boy, a version of which, B. Boy, was later added to the Macy's Thanksgiving Day Parade.

Included in the exhibit were a number of items from *Tim Burton's The Nightmare Before Christmas*, such as a 33x22-inch large-format instant-film photograph of a random stack of body parts from the Sally puppet; an ink and crayon drawing of the early "vamp" version of Sally, with her legs separated from her body and holding her severed arm in the air; an acrylic on black velvet painting of Corpse Boy, with his eyes sewn shut and a sardonic grin, set against a background of question marks; and ink, marker, and colored pencil storyboard panels of Jack wandering into the woods where he would discover Christmas Town.

The private opening for Burton's invited guests was on November 16, 2009. For the museum staff, the opening was the conclusion of a process that had kept them busy for nearly four years. Burton was appreciative. "I feel they did a good job," he said at the celebrity-studded event. "It's kind of chaotic, and fun, which I think is . . . appropriate for the work."

The exhibit garnered positive reviews, and following its five-month run in New York, it moved on to Melbourne, Los Angeles, Toronto, Paris, and Seoul.

OOGIE BOOGIE'S SONG

Well, well, well,
What have we here?
Sandy Claws, huh?
Oooo, I'm really scared
So you're the one everybody's talkin' about?

You're jokin', you're jokin'
I can't believe my eyes
You're jokin' me, you gotta be
This can't be the right guy
He's ancient, he's ugly
I don't know which is worse
I might just split a seam now
If I don't die laughin' first

Sandy Claws, huh? Ohhh, I'm really scared..."

OOGIE (O.S.): "So you're the one everybody's talkin' about...
Ha, ha, ha, ha..."

Tim Burton's The Nightmare Before Christmas *was made for an estimated $18 million, a modest budget compared to the cost of a traditional Disney animated film at the time. It had its theatrical release on October 29, 1993, just in time for Halloween.* Nightmare *initially made $77 million at the box office and garnered positive reviews. But some parents felt the movie was too scary for children. "It was like, 'Wait a minute,'" Burton said. "'If you show it to a bunch of kids without their parents it's great, but as soon as you get the parents involved, you get 'This is too scary.' It's a very disturbing phenomenon."*

When Mister Oogie Boogie says
There's trouble close at hand
You'd better pay attention now
'Cause I'm the Boogie man
And if you aren't a-shakin'
There's something very wrong
'Cause this may be the last time
You hear the Boogie song

Whoa-ohhhh, whoa-oh
Whoa-ohhhh, whoa-oh
Whoa-oh, whoa-oh
I'm the Oogie Boogie Man

Release me now
Or you must face
The dire consequences
The children are expecting me
So please come to your senses

Ha, you're jokin', you're jokin'
I can't believe my ears
Would someone shut this fella up
I'm drownin' in my tears
It's funny, I'm laughin'
You really are too much
And now with your permission

I'm going to do my stuff
Well, what are you going to do?

I'm gonna do the best I can

Whoooa, the sound of rollin' dice to me
Is music in the air
'Cause I'm a gamblin' Boogie Man
Although I don't play fair

It's much more fun, I must confess,
When lives are on the line
Not mine, of course, but yours, old boy,
Now that'd be just fine

Release me fast or you will have to
Answer for this heinous act

Oh, brother, you're something
You put me in a spin
You aren't comprehending
The position that you're in

It's hopeless, you're finished
You haven't got a prayer
'Cause I'm Mister Oogie Boogie
And you ain't going nowhere

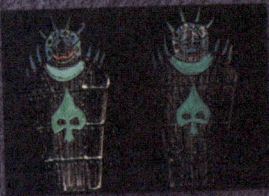

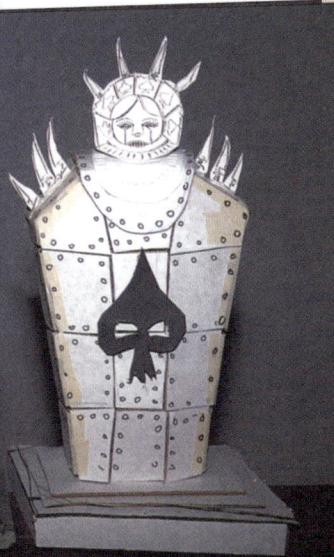

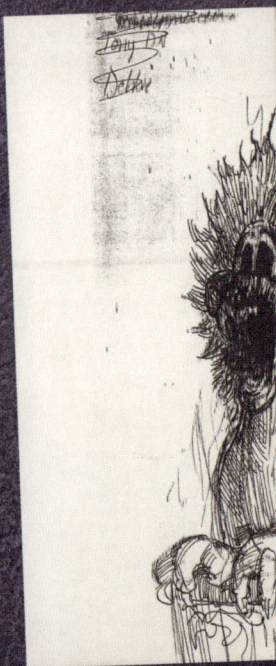

gate to
town square

ART DIRECTION

The art department is where initial sketches are transformed into realized concepts. Art Director Deane Taylor and his three artists worked from the storyboards and, more importantly, from the style defined by Tim Burton's original drawings. "Tim's style is so distinct, so locked down and worked out," Taylor said. "We try not to lose any of that feeling but instead try to work with it and enhance it."

Visual Consultant Rick Heinrichs helped train the artists. "Part of my job . . . was teaching everybody how to be Tim Burton," he said. "Some of the [artists] would draw with the wrong hand so they could learn how to draw in Tim's style."

That technique resulted in a more unstable style that embraced Burton's original vision for the film. "That's when I started getting it," artist Kelly Asbury said. "It made everything just a little unsound."

The artists used medium-point felt-tipped pens, Burton's preferred drawing tool, to create the original line drawings for sets and props. After approval, the artists used markers and colored pencils to try out various color schemes on photocopies. Although the artists drew in two dimensions, they had to think and visualize for a three-dimensional world. Every aspect, from set designs and props to the color palette and lighting details, were considered as if working in three dimensions. Completed designs were faxed to Burton on the set of *Batman Returns*, which he was directing at the time. Taylor learned that if he didn't hear back, the designs were okay. Once approved, detailed illustrations were done and handed off to the set builders, who would then construct a quarter-scale mockup.

While working on *Tim Burton's The Nightmare Before Christmas*, there was no lull in the ideas coming from the artists. One thought led to another and another in an ongoing, energetic exchange of ideas. An example of the various incarnations of a single prop is the iron maiden, a torture device found in Oogie Boogie's gambling lair. The entire art department contributed to its development as it moved from early concept renderings, sketches, color tests, and physical models to the final prop.

However, the most complicated task the art directors had was creating the very different locales in which the story's action takes place. Inspiration was again drawn from Burton's drawings and combined with influences from German Expressionism to give Halloween Town its irregular shapes and edgy, off-kilter look. Christmas Town's candy colors and whimsical joyfulness harkens to Dr. Seuss, Burton's favorite children's author. Inspiration for the scenes set in the real world came from a kind of mash-up of Bauhaus and mid-twentieth-century modernism, which give the suburban real-world settings sharp, straight lines and pastel colors.

Even cave paintings were studied to help create Oogie Boogie's nighttime lair, using black lights and ultra-violet paints. Ancient glowing images of skeletons, spiders, bats, ghosts, and goblins also informed the choreography of Oogie Boogie's dance sequence.

The sets on a three-dimensional stop-motion project have to do more than just look good. There are technical considerations the artists must consider, too. Where can the lighting be placed to create the desired atmosphere? Will the animators be able to easily reach every point on the set in order to do their jobs? There was tight collaboration between the artists and the set builders to make sure things were being realized as planned. With a lot of planning and design, questions were answered and problems were solved before the cameras clicked off their frames. But still, the artists were never truly finished with their work until a scene was fully approved and the set was no longer needed.

Camera holds as Oogie Boogie smirks at Santa Claus.

Oogie Boogie laughs.

INT. TREEHOUSE - NIGHT

Lock, Shock, and Barrel listen at the mouth of the mask and
react with delight.

Lock, Shock, and Barrel laugh.

EXT. HALLOWEEN TOWN SQUARE - NIGHT

The Mayor, with his optimistic face turned forward, leads the
skeleton band in a dirge-like rendition of "Jingle Bells."
Creatures crowd the square to listen.

(Overlapping, low, and indistinct chatter and laughter continues
          under the following scenes and dialogue)

Sally steps toward the fountain, then she looks around
cautiously. Sally opens the jug of fog juice, then she pours the
fog juice into the fountain. Fog rises up out of the fountain.

The Mayor conducts the skeleton band. Camera tilts up and
slightly off the Mayor and the skeleton band to reveal a coffin,
forming the body of a sleigh, which is on a platform. The coffin
opens and Jack, dressed in his Santa Claus outfit, rises up out
of it. Jack waves at the creatures. The creatures look at Jack
and applaud excitedly. Sally enters, then she walks and pretends
to join in the applause.

The Mayor walks up some steps to the platform, camera tilting
up with him to reveal Jack's sleigh, which is on the platform,
and the skeleton reindeer, who are ready to pull it. The Mayor
pulls a sheet of paper out of his pocket and begins to make a
speech.

                         MAYOR
                    (optimistic face)
Think of us as you soar triumphantly through the sky,
outshining every star . . .

MAKING PUPPETS

The origin of the design that became *Tim Burton's The Nightmare Before Christmas* emanated from the initial sketches Tim Burton made when writing his original poem some ten years before actual production of the film began in 1991. However, no matter how inspirational and well thought out those drawings were, there were times when what was on paper could not be exactly translated by the puppet makers into a functional three-dimensional form. Adjustments had to be made so the puppet could move as needed to meet the demands of the action described in the script and mapped out by the storyboard artists. Balancing Burton's conceptual vision with the realities of constructing a puppet the animators could work with was a recurring challenge for puppet makers.

"If you look at the original drawings of Jack Skellington by Burton, Jack was twice as skinny as what we ended up shooting," said Eric Leighton, supervising animator. "We were at our limits; we've made him skinny, but we stopped where it was impossible."

While Burton was widely considered an easy, collaborative partner, there were times when a bit of discussion and compromise was needed. Director Henry Selick remembered a discussion with him about Sally's thin ankles not working with her fuller body. Selick's suggestion was to give Sally socks to hide the need for her to have more robust ankles so her legs could be thin. Burton wasn't so sure. "Tim agonized for a couple of days," Selick recalled, "and finally said, 'Okay, if she has stripes on her socks, I can buy that.'"

Jack smiles smugly.

                    MAYOR (CONT'D)
                  (optimistic face)
. . . your silhouette a dark blot on the moon.

Fog pours out of the fountain.

                    MAYOR (CONT'D)
                  (optimistic face)
You, who are our pride. You, who are our glory. You, who
have frightened millions into an early grave.

The skeleton band looks at the Mayor as fog begins to obscure
them. The saxophone player looks at the fog with surprise.

                 SAXOPHONE PLAYER
    Huh?

The Mayor reads his speech as the fog floats into frame.

                      MAYOR
                  (optimistic face)
You who have, uh, devastated the, the souls of
    the living . . .

Jack looks at the fog with dismay.

                      JACK
    Oh, no. We can't take off in this. The reindeer can't see
an inch in front of their noses.

(Overlapping, indistinct chatter and expressions of confusion
  and dismay continues under following scenes and dialogue)

                      SALLY
    Whew!

Sally wipes her brow with relief. Camera moves past Cyclops to
two vampires, who stand and look glumly at the fog.

                              VAMPIRE #1
            The fog's thick as, as . . .

                              CYCLOPS
            Jellied brains.

                              VAMPIRE #2
            Or thicker.

Jack sits down in the sleigh and rubs his head with dismay.
Camera moves across the creatures, who look sadly at Jack.

                              JACK
            There go all of my hopes . . . my precious plans . . . my
            glorious dreams.

                              CORPSE CHILD
            There goes Christmas.

The Corpse Child starts to cry. Jack sits glumly
in the sleigh.

Zero barks.

Jack shakes his head.

                              JACK
            No, Zero. Down, boy.

Jack looks up with sudden realization, then he looks at Zero.

                              JACK (CONT'D)
            My, what a brilliant . . .

Zero floats in the air as his nose glows red.

                              JACK (CONT'D)
            . . . nose you have. The better to light my way!

Sally, standing amidst the creatures, reacts with dismay.

· CORPSE CHILD

JACK (CONT'D)

B41 B42 B42 ∅

B43 B44 B45 ∅

B46 B47 B48 B51 B46

B52 B53 B54 B55 ∅

B56 B57 B58 B61 B62

TRYING TO SEE EYE TO EYE

The eyes are windows to the soul, as the saying goes, and every animator understands that well-drawn eyes can evoke empathy in a character, while poorly executed eyes can make them unrelatable.

Tim Burton fully understood this principle when he designed Jack Skellington with two black holes where his eyes should've been. But Burton enjoyed the challenge of bringing to life an eyeless skeleton. "It was funny to think of a character that had these big black holes and to try and make that work," Burton said. When Burton and his team pitched the project as a stop-motion animated film to Disney Studio in the late 1980s, the issue came up immediately. "That was . . . their first comment, you know, 'You need eyes,'" Burton said with a laugh.

"But that was the point. That was the challenge the animators and everyone took on board. And, [in the end] it was great. But that was definitely almost a deal-breaker."

To compensate for the lack of expressive eyeballs, animators managed to convey emotion by having Jack blink and manipulating his eye sockets, changing their shape in sync with his facial expressions.

        To the head of the team, Zero.

The creatures begin to become excited. Zero floats through
the air.

        (Overlapping, indistinct, excited chatter continues under
                following scenes and dialogue)

The Corpse Child smiles at Zero. Jack, sitting in the sleigh,
picks up the reins.

                        JACK (CONT'D)
        We're off!

Looking past the crowd to the skeleton reindeer, who stand
on the platform with Zero in the lead. The reindeer pull Jack
into frame. Sally pushes through the crowd, then she gestures
frantically at Jack.

                        SALLY
        Wait, Jack, no!

The skeleton reindeer pull Jack, sitting in the sleigh, up into
the air and exit. The creatures look up at Jack and cheer.
Camera reveals Sally, who stands in the crowd and folds her
hands with despair.

The skeleton reindeer pull Jack, sitting in the sleigh, through
the sky.

                        JACK
        Ho, ho, ho! Ha, ha, ha, ha, hooo!

Sally, standing amidst the creatures, stares sadly at off-screen
Jack. The creatures exit in all directions as the crowd
disperses. Sally waves at Jack.

                        SALLY
        Good-bye, Jack. My dearest Jack. Oh, how
        I hope my premonition is wrong.

Sally walks.

SALLY'S SONG

I sense there's something in the wind
That feels like tragedy's at hand
And though I'd like to stand by him
Can't shake this feeling that I have
The worst is just around the bend

And does he notice my feelings for him?
And will he see how much he means to me?
I think it's not to be

What will become of my dear friend?
Where will his actions lead us then?
Although I'd like to join the crowd
In their enthusiastic cloud
Try as I may, it doesn't last

And will we ever end up together?
No, I think not, it's never to become
For I am not the one

GETTING THE SCRIPT "WRITE"

With production on the film already underway, Tim Burton hired Caroline Thompson to write his story's screenplay. Before she came on board, another Burton collaborator, Michael McDowell, had begun working on the script. "The original draft had some good ideas but was not completely successful," Director Henry Selick said.

Burton had also been working closely with composer Danny Elfman who, by the time Thompson was brought in, had completed about 80 percent of the songs, some of which had gone to the storyboarding stage. "My objective was to write a story to thread all these songs together," Thompson said. "And to fill out characters who weren't otherwise filled out."

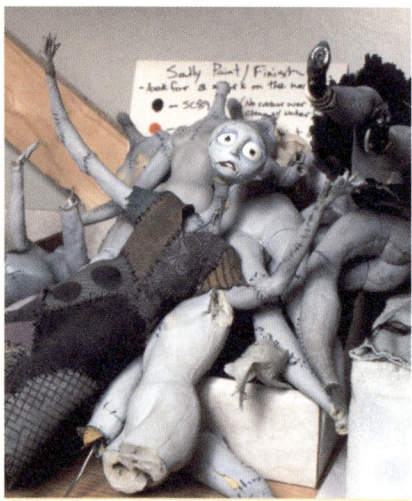

Setting the McDowell script aside, Thompson took herself to a house on the beach and began writing based on the content in the songs. Her first challenge was to meld together Burton's fanciful drawings and Elfman's storytelling lyrics. But once she got started, the words flowed. Just two weeks later, she handed in the script. Burton was pleased, as Thompson clearly understood what he was going for. Burton made only four small notes on the script. There were no revisions.

One of Thompson's challenges was the development of Sally's character. Burton's original sketches depicted her as something of a vamp, which Thompson couldn't relate to. She had imagined Sally to be a more fragile character who, through the story, would be able to show just how tough she really was. Her reinterpretation of Sally prompted a redesign of the character, and Sally became more stick-like, with a dress of stitched-together rags. Thompson liked the new look. "I could understand her narrative better than when she was just this full-blown babe," she said. When all was said and done, Thompson was proud of the work she had done shaping Sally's personality. "Her story . . . was my primary contribution to the film," she said.

Working on the script ". . . required a lot of flexibility," Thompson said. Given the evolutionary process of making an animated film, there is a great deal of give and take. Thompson remarked that it was not uncommon for the script to be torn apart by storyboard artists, who would give back drawings with notes. In consultation with Burton, she would then rework the script.

"Yet, even with all this back and forth, the basic structure of the script remained what I gave them," she said. Thompson was much more involved in the making of the film than a live-action screenwriter would be. It was an ongoing process that continued throughout every stage of the production.

"I could never really sleep at night," Thompson said. "I couldn't just say, 'Well, that's done.' It was a very long process for everybody."

Commenting on the finished film, Director Henry Selick said, "Tim's basic story is elegant, simple, and strong." Thompson agreed and added, "The film's sophistication is, ironically, in its simplicity. It's Jack's journey. He learns to recognize his own strengths. There's definitely a lesson to be learned. Be true to thyself. That's where our joys are."

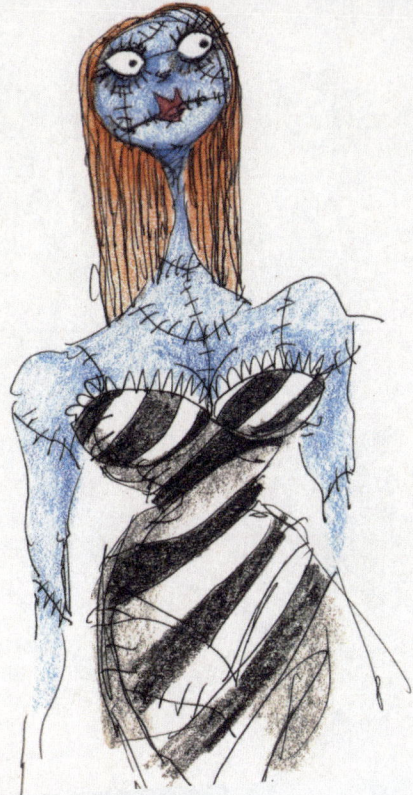

THIS CONCEPT ART shows stages in the development of Sally. The line art of her head, face, and hair are early explorations of her basic look. The two color drawings show her reconceptualization from a vamp to a waif. The final drawing is a concept art piece for the film, attributed to artist Kendal Cronkhite. The other drawings were done by Disney Studio Artists.

Camera looks through gate to the skeleton band, who hang
their heads as they finish playing the song.

EXT. SKY - NIGHT

Jack sits in the sleigh, camera moving with him as the
reindeer pull him. Camera moves in through the clouds to
reveal the lighted houses of Suburbia, which are below.
Jack sits in the sleigh, camera moving with him as the
skeleton reindeer pull him. Jack flails the reins to make
the skeleton reindeer move faster. Zero leads the skeleton
reindeer down toward Suburbia.

Camera moves down toward the lighted statues of angels,
which are atop the roof of Timmie's house.

INT. TIMMIE'S HOUSE/BEDROOM - NIGHT

Timmie, a small boy, sleeps in his bed. The crunch of Jack's
sleigh landing on the roof is heard. One of the lighted
angels, visible through a window, drops down into frame.
Timmie wakes up.

                         TIMMIE
          Santa!

EXT. TIMMIE'S HOUSE - NIGHT

Jack stands up in his sleigh, which is atop the roof, and
pulls out his bag of toys. Jack walks to the chimney, then
he leaps into the chimney and exits.

INT. TIMMIE'S HOUSE/STAIRCASE - NIGHT

Looking through a hallway door to Timmie, who enters.
Timmie then hurries down the stairs.

From Timmie's point of view, camera dollies in down the
staircase and through the foyer, then pans to reveal Jack,
who stands in the living room and opens his sack beside
the Christmas tree.

Timmie gasps.

Camera holds as Jack reaches into his sack.

INT. TIMMIE'S HOUSE/LIVING ROOM - NIGHT

Looking through the foyer doorway to Timmie, who peers at Jack.
Timmie tiptoes into the living room.

Camera dollies in as Jack fills the Christmas stockings, which
are hung on the fireplace.

> TIMMIE
> Santa?

Jack looks around with surprise. Then he leans down and looks at
Timmie. Timmie looks at him with fright.

> JACK
> Merry Christmas! And what is your name?

> TIMMIE
> Uh . . . uh, uh, uh, uh . . .

> JACK
> That's all right. I have a special present for you anyway.

Jack reaches into his sack, then he pulls out a Christmas present
and holds it toward Timmie. Jack's hand, reaching in, hands the
present to Timmie. Jack's hand exits.

> JACK (CONT'D)
> There you go, sonny.

Timmie looks up unsurely at Jack. Jack stands upside down in the
chimney and looks at Timmie.

> JACK (CONT'D)
> Ho, ho, ho, ho, ha . . . ha . . . haaa.

Jack exits up the chimney. Timmie stares up at the chimney.
Timmie looks down quizzically at the gift package. Timmie opens
the present and stares down into it. Timmie's mother (feet) and
Timmie's father (feet) enter and walk toward Timmie.

> MOTHER
> And what did Santa bring you, honey?

Camera looks past Father and Mother to Timmie, who turns and looks at them. Timmie pulls a shrunken head up out of the box.

>   MOTHER & FATHER
>   (overlapping screams)

EXT. TIMMIE'S HOUSE - NIGHT

The skeleton reindeer pull Jack, sitting in the sleigh, through the sky.

>   MOTHER & FATHER (OFF)
>   (overlapping screams)

>   JACK
>   Merry Christmas!

INT. POLICE STATION - NIGHT

Two street lights with lamps are on either side of the front desk of a police station. The lettering on the lamps reads: Police. A police sergeant sits at the desk. A telephone on the desk rings. The police sergeant answers the telephone.

>   POLICE SERGEANT
>   (into phone)
>   Hello. Police.

>   WOMAN CALLER
>   (over telephone)
>   (indistinct, hysterical shouts)

>   POLICE SERGEANT
>   (into telephone)
>   Attacked by Christmas toys? That's strange. That's the second
>   complaint we've had.

EXT. SKY - NIGHT

Jack, sitting in the sleigh, is pulled by the reindeer, camera moving with him as he looks down at Suburbia. Jack laughs.

The sleigh starts to descend, camera moving down with it.

INT. HALLOWEEN TOWN SQUARE - NIGHT

The Witches and several other creatures crowd around the
Witches' cauldron, which shows an image of Jack as he flies
through the sky in his sleigh.

CROWD
(overlapping laughter)

INT. GRANNY'S HOUSE - NIGHT

A shadow of Granny, who rocks in her rocking chair, is on
the wall. Jack, visible through a window, enters, then he peers
through the window. Jack hurries and exits. A door opens to
again reveal Jack, who hangs a Killer Wreath on the door. Jack
then closes the door and obscures himself.

Eyes appear on the Killer Wreath, which hangs on the door.

The Killer Wreath snarls. The Killer Wreath glares at off-
screen Granny.

INT. HOUSE/LIVING ROOM - NIGHT

A Christmas tree is in the background. Jack enters, then he
crosses and stops. He lowers his bag into frame, then a huge
snake slithers out of it. The snake slithers and curls around
the base of the Christmas tree. Jack hurries and exits.

INT. WANDA'S HOUSE/LIVING ROOM - NIGHT

A Christmas tree is in the background. Jack enters, then he
puts some toys down under the tree. Wanda and Ronnie, two small
African-American children, enter and walk. They stop and stare
at the toys under the tree.

                    WANDA
     Come on.

Ronnie chuckles.

Wanda and Ronnie hurry toward the tree. Wanda stops and picks
up a doll as Ronnie hurries toward a gift box.

                    WANDA (CONT'D)
     Wait.

Ronnie stops and lifts up the gift box to reveal the Evil Toy Duck. The Evil Toy Duck turns and glares at Ronnie. The doll snaps its teeth at Wanda.

The Evil Toy Duck quacks. Ronnie and Wanda scream. Ronnie and Wanda run and exit. The doll and the Evil Toy Duck chase after the children.

INT. WANDA'S HOUSE - NIGHT

Looking down the staircase to the foyer.

Ronnie screams.

                    WANDA (OFF)
                      Mom!

Ronnie and Wanda enter and run up the staircase.

                    RONNIE
                   Mom! Dad!

                    WANDA
                    Dad!

Ronnie and Wanda exit. The Evil Toy Duck enters and chases after them.

                    RONNIE (OFF)
                     Help!

                    WANDA (OFF)
                   Hellllp!

EXT. WANDA'S HOUSE/CHILDREN'S BEDROOM - NIGHT

Looking through the hallway doorway to Wanda and Ronnie, who run into the bedroom. Ronnie screams. Wanda slams the door behind them and holds it closed.

EXT. SUBURBIA - NIGHT

Jack enters and leaps onto the roof of a house. He drops a present down a chimney. Jack jumps onto a second house, camera moving with him. A light goes on inside the first house.

Man inside house #1 screams.

Jack drops a present down a the chimney of the second house, then he leaps onto the roof of a third house. A light goes on in the second house.

Woman inside house #2 screams.

Jack drops a present down a the chimney of the third house.

INT. HOUSE/LIVING ROOM - NIGHT

Two children look at a Christmas tree. Bats suddenly fly out of the Christmas tree.

The children scream and run.

INT. GRANNY'S HOUSE - NIGHT

The Killer Wreath hangs on the door as Granny's shadow is on the wall. Strands of the Killer Wreath run down out of frame, then the shadow
of the wreath's strand appears on the wall as it moves toward Granny.

Granny (in shadow) screams.

INT. HOUSE - NIGHT

A boy screams as the snake eats the Christmas tree.

INT. HOWIE'S HOUSE/HALLWAY - NIGHT

Howie, a chubby boy, enters, then flees down the hallway. A Jack-in-the-box enters, then hops after him. The Jack-in-the-box laughs malevolently.

INT. HOUSE - NIGHT

Parents slide a sofa and cabinet in front of the fireplace, blocking it.

INT. ANOTHER HOUSE - NIGHT

A mother enters, then she locks the front door.

STEEL SKELETONS

Every character in *Tim Burton's The Nightmare Before Christmas* had an armature (framework) made out of steel or aluminum and/or wire. The armatures provide total support for a puppet yet allow it to move naturally and to steadfastly hold a pose. The structures were precision built with metal rods, swivel joints, ball joints, hinges, and screws. Some armatures required hundreds of such parts. There were no off-the-shelf parts available for the armatures; every piece was handcrafted at the studio.

The first step in building an armature was to define how a character would move and design a mechanism that would facilitate those movements. When it came to posing, the armature had to be engineered to tighten down the joints, especially the ankles, and hold a pose indefinitely. Any sudden jump in movement, known as a "pop," could be a shot killer, meaning the entire sequence would have to be redone.

Most of the armatures on *Nightmare* were designed by Tom St. Amand, who was, simply, "the best in the business," according to his colleague, Armature Maker Blair Clark.

Before working on *Nightmare*, St. Amand already had a long and impressive background in building armatures for major motion pictures and commercials. But a unique challenge presented on the *Nightmare* project was that many of Burton's character designs had full bodies, skinny ankles, and tiny feet. Given the nature of stop-motion production and the lack of any digital editing capabilities in the early 1990s, the puppets could not have additional supports or wires to help them stand. Everything had to rely on the metal armature inside.

Director Henry Selick was concerned that building an armature for Jack Skellington would be challenging because of his long, thin frame. And, while there were engineering problems to solve, St. Amand and his crew succeeded with the difficult task.

"[St. Amand] was able to make the smallest ankles, the smallest feet that were still able to support Jack's height," Selick said. "Any lesser armature maker would not have been able to pull it off; Jack would have been much thicker, much chunkier looking."

St. Amand was pleased with the result as well but admitted that Jack "was a little harder to animate because you'd have to really tighten down tight on the ankle joints." St. Amand and his team constructed a total of eighteen Jack armatures so the puppet could be used on multiple stages simultaneously.

In contrast, Sculptor Norm DeCarlo recalled, "You could tow a truck with Oogie's armature!" Even though Oogie Boogie's armature had to be big and bulky to support the very large character, he also had to dance—slinking, sliding, and undulating—during his song. To accomplish this, Clark made "pushers," which are little metal rods with blunted ends that could be used to manipulate Oogie Boogie's torso.

Interestingly, armatures were not just for puppets. Case in point is Spiral Hill, which unfurls as Jack walks down it singing "Jack's Lament" in the film's first act. Inside the flexible spiral is a steel and wire armature that allows the hill to unwind one frame at a time in sync with Jack's movements.

Armature building is exacting work. On *Tim Burton's The Nightmare Before Christmas*, multiple armatures had to be built for each character. "Over one hundred armatures were made for this show," Clark marveled. "Just insane!"

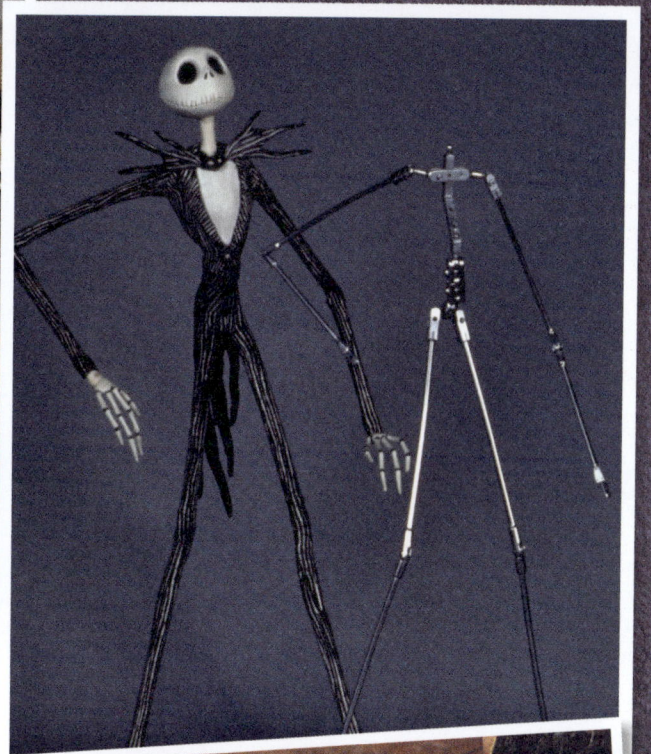

INT. ANOTHER HOUSE - NIGHT

A father closes the shutters on a
window and locks them.

INT. ANOTHER HOUSE - NIGHT

A father enters and locks a door.

INT. ANOTHER HOUSE - NIGHT

A father closes the shutters on a fireplace. He then drops a bar
across the shutters and locks them.

INT. ANOTHER HOUSE - NIGHT

A father's hand enters and turns up the flames in the fireplace.

EXT. SUBURBIA - NIGHT

Jack enters and crosses across a roof.

                         JACK
          You're welcome one and all!

INT. POLICE STATION - NIGHT

The police sergeant sits at his desk and talks into a telephone
receiver. He now has several telephones on his desk and they are
all ringing.

                    POLICE SERGEANT
                    (into telephone)
          Where'd you spot him? Fast as we can, ma'am.

The police sergeant hangs up the telephone receiver, then he
picks up the receiver of a second telephone.

                 POLICE SERGEANT (CONT'D)
                    (into telephone)
          Police. I know, I know. A skeleton. Keep calm. Turn off
          all the lights. Make sure the doors are locked.

The police sergeant hangs up the second telephone, then he picks
up the receiver of a third telephone.

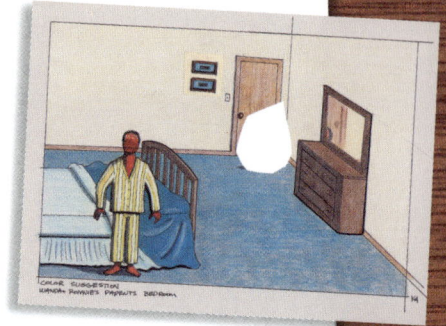

                    POLICE SERGEANT (CONT'D)
                       (into telephone)
        Hello, police.

INT. RADIO STATION - NIGHT

A female radio announcer reads from a sheet of copy. A sign reads:
On Air.

                    FEMALE RADIO ANNOUNCER
                    (reading into microphone)
        Reports are pouring in from all over the globe that an
        imposter is shamelessly impersonating . . .

INT. HALLOWEEN TOWN SQUARE - NIGHT

Sally stands as she, the Witches, and other creatures peer down into
the Witches' cauldron.

                    FEMALE RADIO ANNOUNCER
                       (over speaker)
        . . . Santa Claus, mocking and mangling this joyous holiday.
        The authorities assure us that at this moment . . .

The Witches and the creatures cheer as Sally reacts nervously.
Sally looks down nervously into the cauldron.

           (Overlapping cheers continue under following)

                  FEMALE RADIO ANNOUNCER (CONT'D)
                       (over speaker)
        . . . military units are mobilizing to stop the perpetrator of
this heinous crime.

Sally looks up and reacts with concern.

                            SALLY
        Jack. Someone has to help Jack.

                    FEMALE RADIO ANNOUNCER
                       (over speaker)
        Santa Claus, wherever you are, come back.

Sally looks at the Witches and the creatures, who stand around the cauldron.

                    SALLY
        Where'd they take that Sandy Claws?

                FEMALE RADIO ANNOUNCER
                    (over speaker)
        Come back and save Christmas . . .

The Witches and creatures ignore Sally, who hurries away.

EXT. MILITARY INSTALLATION - NIGHT

A siren sounds atop some hangers. A radar scope spins. Searchlights turn on and are aimed up into the sky.

EXT. SKY - NIGHT

The skeleton reindeer pull Jack, sitting in the sleigh, camera moving with them. The light from the searchlights hit the sleigh.

                    JACK
        Look, Zero.

EXT. MILITARY INSTALLATION - NIGHT

Looking down at the military installation as searchlights scan the sky.

                    JACK
        Searchlights.

EXT. MILITARY INSTALLATION - NIGHT

A gunner turns the wheel of a cannon. The barrels of several cannons rise into the air, then they fire missiles up at off-screen Jack.

EXT. SKY - NIGHT

The skeleton reindeer pull Jack, sitting in the sleigh, camera moving with them. Zero leads the sleigh. Missiles start to explode around the sleigh. Jack smiles as the skeleton reindeer pull the sleigh.

JACK

  They're celebrating. They're thanking us for doing such a
good job.

Zero flies through the air, camera moving with him. A missile
explodes, sending Zero tumbling through the air. Jack looks
down toward the ground.

JACK (CONT'D)

  Whoa! Careful down there. You almost hit us.

Zeros barks.

Jack looks at Zero.

JACK (CONT'D)

  It's okay, Zero. Head higher.

Zero barks.

Zero starts to fly up higher into the sky. Zero leads the
skeleton reindeer up toward a cloud. Zero, the skeleton
reindeer, and Jack exit into the cloud.

INT. OOGIE BOOGIE'S DUNGEON - NIGHT

A pair of dice lay on the floor. Oogie Boogie's hand enters and
picks up the dice.

OOGIE BOOGIE

  Are you a gamblin' man . . .

Oogie Boogie looks at Santa Claus, who hangs from a hook.

OOGIE BOOGIE (CONT'D)

  . . . Sandy? Let's play!

Oogie Boogie shakes the dice in Santa Claus's face. The sound of
a door opening is heard.

OOGIE BOOGIE (CONT'D)

  Hmm?

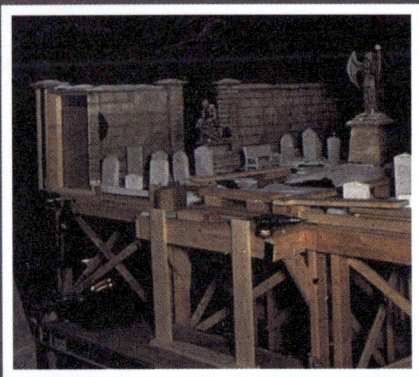

SETS

Every set for *Tim Burton's The Nightmare Before Christmas* had to be strong enough to withstand the weight of an animator should he or she need to crawl onto it to manipulate a puppet. To support them, as well as the set pieces and scenery, the table-height sets had to be extremely solid to avoid jiggling, slipping, or moving as the scene was being shot. "If the set doesn't hold up, it may be twelve or fourteen hours' work for the animator down the drain," said Bo Henry, set construction supervisor for the film.

To avoid such a disaster, the design and construction team built a scale model for every set drawing they received. The model was built to work out any issues that may arise during filming. The scale of things on a stop-motion production like *Nightmare* was different than on a live-action set. For example, a light couldn't be hidden behind a set piece, since, often, the light itself was way too big. Everything had to be planned out and precisely orchestrated so there were no surprises. To assist the animators, who preferred to have no more than two and a half feet between them and their puppet, sizable sets, like Halloween Town, were constructed so that sections could be pulled out. Trap doors were also used so that animators could work in areas that would otherwise be inaccessible. Even with these built-in features, there were many times when animators had to crawl up onto the set to do their work. That's when the set's sturdy construction paid off the most.

With multiple sets working at the same time, Set Builder Fon Davis recalled that there was little down time in the scene shop. "We built a set and a half per week for two and a half years!" Davis said.

Oogie Boogie turns and looks. Sally's leg sticks through the door.

>   OOGIE BOOGIE (CONT'D)
>   My, my. What have we here?

Santa Claus hangs on the hook as Oogie Boogie stares at Sally's off-screen leg. Oogie Boogie spits on his hand. Oogie Boogie slicks back the top of his head, then he walks.

Oogie Boogie grunts.

Sally's hands, which she has pulled off her body, enter, then they fly and grab hold of a rope. Sally's hands slide down the rope, camera tilting down with them to reveal the hook. Camera tilts down, off Sally's hands and the hook, to reveal Santa Claus. Camera holds as Sally's hands reenter, then they drop down onto Santa Claus's beard. Santa Claus gasps. Sally's hands clasp down over Santa Claus's mouth, then they point up. Sally's torso leans through a window and looks down at Santa Claus.

>   SALLY
>   (whispering)
>   I'll get you out of here.

Oogie Boogie leans toward Sally's leg.

>   OOGIE BOOGIE
>   Ah, lovely.

Oogie Boogie pulls the shoe off the leg and tickles the sole of the foot.

>   OOGIE BOOGIE (CONT'D)
>   Tickle, tickle, tickle.

Sally's hands untie the rope that binds Santa Claus to the hook.

>   OOGIE BOOGIE (CONT'D) (OFF)
>   Tickle, tickle, tickle.

Santa Claus drops to the ground as Sally lowers a rope ladder from the window.

OOGIE BOOGIE (CONT'D) (OFF)
Tickle, tickle, tickle. (in falsetto) Tickle, tickle, tickle.

Santa Claus turns toward the rope ladder. Oogie Boogie holds Sally's leg and tickles it. Oogie Boogie chuckles. Oogie Boogie pulls Sally's leg through the doorway, then he suddenly realizes it is not attached to anything.

OOGIE BOOGIE (CONT'D)
What! You try to make a dupe out of meeee?!

Santa Claus climbs up the rope ladder toward Sally, who stands in the window. Sally's hands climb up the rope. Oogie Boogie roars toward Santa Claus. Santa Claus hangs onto the rope ladder and Sally hangs onto the window as Oogie Boogie tries to suck them. Sally's hands try to hold onto the rope, but then they are sucked out of frame. Santa Claus is sucked out of frame, then Sally loses her hold on the window. Sally is sucked out of frame.

EXT. SKY - NIGHT

The skeleton reindeer pull Jack, sitting in the sleigh, camera moving with them. Zero leads them. Jack lifts a list into frame and looks at it.

JACK
Who's next on my list?

Jack holds up a list which reads: Oliver, Harry, Jordan, Allison, Kevin, Kayla.

JACK (CONT'D)
Ah, little Harry and Jordan. Won't they be surprised?

The skeleton reindeer pull Jack from behind the cloud cover and across the face of the moon. The searchlights scan the sky for Jack. The reindeer pull Jack, camera moving with him as the searchlights hit the sleigh.

EXT. MILITARY INSTALLATION - NIGHT

The cannon barrels fire missiles up at Jack. A skeleton
reindeer flies, camera moving with it. A missile enters lower
frame, then it hits the skeleton reindeer and knocks off its
head. Jack reacts with surprise. Another missile enters lower
frame and rips through the bag on the back of the sleigh. Jack
reacts with shock.

                    JACK
          They're trying to hit us. Zeroooo!

Zero flies through the air, camera moving with him. Zero turns
and looks plaintively at Jack. Zero barks.

EXT. MILITARY INSTALLATION - NIGHT

A radar screen shows an image of Jack's sleigh directly in
the crosshairs of its sight. A flashing sign above the screen
reads: Armed. A sign below the screen flashes on; it reads: Fire.
A cannon fires a missile at Jack.

EXT. SKY - NIGHT

The missile files up through the air toward Jack. The skeleton
reindeer pull Jack across the sky. Camera moves in toward the
sleigh. The missile flies up toward the off-screen sleigh. The
red blast of an explosion fills the frame. The sleigh breaks
into pieces, sending Jack tumbling through the sky. Jack and
the pieces of the sleigh fall through the air, camera moving
down wtih them to reveal the lights of Suburbia.

                    JACK
          Merry Christmas to all, and to all a good niiiiiiight!

Jack and the pieces of the sleigh hit the ground.

EXT. HALLOWEEN TOWN SQUARE - NIGHT

The Witches' cauldron shows the image of Suburbia. Camera
moves to reveal Cyclops, the Wolfman and the Mayor, with his
pessimistic face, standing and staring down into the cauldron
with horror. The Wolfman leans back his head and howls.

The Mayor shakes his head, then he walks and exits. Witches and creatures stand around the cauldron as the Mayor walks.

                    MAYOR
              (pessimistic face)
     I knew this Christmas thing was a bad idea.
     I felt it in my gut.

The Mayor sits down in his hearse, then lifts a microphone and talks into it.

                  MAYOR (CONT'D)
         (pessimistic face) (into megaphone)
     Terrible news, folks. The worst tragedy of our times.

The Mayor drives the hearse and exits. Camera moves past some creatures, standing, to the Mayor, who drives his hearse.

                  MAYOR (CONT'D)
         (pessimistic face) (into microphone)
     Jack has been blown to smithereens. Terrible,
     terrible news.

The Vampires and some other creatures enter, then they hang their heads sadly.

EXT. SUBURBIA STREETS - NIGHT

A policeman, sitting in his police car, drives the car, camera moving with him. The logo on car door reads: Police. The policeman lifts a microphone and talks into it.

                   POLICEMAN
                 (over speaker)
         Attention. Attention, citizens.

Looking through a window to Timmie, who pushes back the curtain and looks at the off-screen policeman.

                POLICEMAN (CONT'D)
                 (over speaker)
         Terrible news.

Camera looking through the open doorway of a house to a child, who cries and holds onto his father.

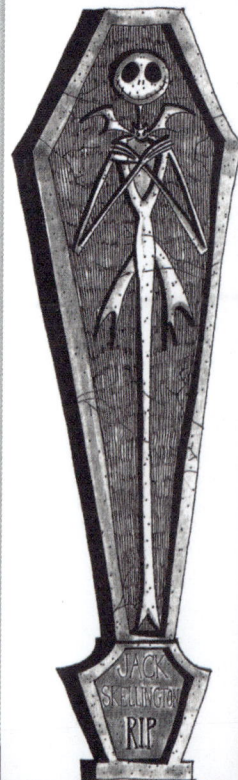

                    POLICEMAN (CONT'D)
                    (over speaker)
     There's still no . . .

Camera looking through a window to two little girls, who stand
beside their mother and cry.

                    POLICEMAN (CONT'D)
                    (over speaker)
     . . . sign of Santa Claus.

The policeman drives the police car, camera dollying with him.

                    POLICEMAN (CONT'D)
                    (over speaker)
     Although the impostor has been . . .

EXT. SUBURBIA CEMETERY - NIGHT

Camera cranes down to reveal the fragments of the sleigh, which
lay in the cemetery and burn.

                    POLICEMAN (OFF)
                    (over speaker)
     . . . shot down, it looks like Christmas will have to be
     canceled this year. I repeat, the impostor has been shot
     down, but there's still no sign of the real Santa.

Camera moves past Jack, lying in the arms of the statue of
an angel, to the sleigh, which lays on the ground amidst the
gravestones.

Camera dollies and pans around the statue to fully reveal Jack.
Zero enters, then he flies toward Jack and looks at him woefully.
Zero carries Jack's teeth in his mouth, then he puts the teeth
down in Jack's mouth.

Zero whines.

Camera continues to dolly as Jack sits up in the arms of the
statue.

POOR JACK

What have I done?
What have I done?
How could I be so blind?
All is lost, where was I?
Spoiled all, spoiled all
Everything's gone all wrong

What have I done?
What have I done?
Find a deep cave to hide in
In a million years they'll find me
Only dust and a plaque
That reads "Here lies poor old Jack"

But I never intended all this madness, never
And nobody really understood, well, how could they?
That all I ever wanted was to bring them something great
Why does nothing ever turn out like it should?

Well, what the heck, I went and did my best
And, by God, I really tasted something swell
And for a moment, why, I even touched the sky
And at least I left some stories they can tell, I did

And for the first time since I don't remember when
I felt just like my old bony self again
And I, Jack, the Pumpkin King
That's right, I am the Pumpkin King!

And I just can't wait until next Halloween
'Cause I've got some new ideas that will really make them scream
And, by God, I'm really going to give it all my might
Uh oh, I hope there's still time to set things right
Sandy Claws . . .

RICK HEINRICHS

At the end of a film, when the credits roll, there can be no doubt in anyone's mind that moviemaking is a team sport. You need a lot of people, both in front of and behind the camera, to make a film. If you're one of the talented filmmakers who make up the A-list, you might have the good fortune to assemble a team of people who can jump right into a project because they understand you, your vision, and the way you think. Tim Burton is one of those lucky filmmakers.

Rick Heinrichs, a CalArts graduate like Burton, is an award-winning producer, production designer, special effects artist, and art director. He won an Academy Award in 1999 for art direction on the Burton film *Sleepy Hollow* and has dozens of credits for hits, such as *Star Wars: The Last Jedi*, two *Pirates of the Caribbean* films, and, of course, *Tim Burton's The Nightmare Before Christmas*. In fact, Heinrichs has worked on almost every film Burton has done.

In the early days, while Burton was working on *The Fox and the Hound* at Disney as an in-betweener—an assistant animator who fills in the action between key frames—he was also making notes and drawings for projects he hoped to eventually produce, including early drawings for *Tim Burton's The Nightmare Before Christmas*. One fateful day, Heinrichs decided to pay Burton a visit. "When I actually went into his office and saw the work on the wall, I was just blown away . . . by the concept," he recalled. "So simple, clever, and unique. I immediately did a sculpture of Jack and then a sculpture of Zero after that."

Heinrichs also built 3-D models of Burton's character and prop designs for Disney's next production, *The Black Cauldron*. Although Burton's designs were not used in the film, the work was important in another way, according to Heinrichs. "When we started working together, I realized there was something out of that collaboration that was greater than [the sum of] the parts."

The experience led to Burton and Heinrichs being assigned to a variety of projects, such as designing a puppet show for the Disney Channel and writing a children's book. The book was called "Vincent," and it was based on an original story written by Burton about a little boy who believed he was Vincent Price, the classic star of monster movies. With prior experience in stop-motion animation, Heinrichs suggested they turn the book into a short film. Their supervisor agreed and gave them a small budget to create a stop-motion test film. "We kind of got pulled out of the animation department into a 'special experimental unit,'" Heinrichs said. "And that was really the beginning of our collaboration. Essentially, the evolution of *The Nightmare Before Christmas*, I would say, was the culmination of all that experimentation."

The puppets for both Jack Skellington and Zero were sculpted by Heinrichs from Burton's original sketches. Those same three-dimensional prototypes, with very few modifications, were used as models ten years later when the film went into production. Heinrichs worked on virtually every aspect of the movie and, working from Burton's drawings, was the dominant force in developing the look of Halloween Town. It was a task he greatly enjoyed because, with stop-motion, "You're free to design whatever you want without the limitations imposed by full size and live action," he said.

Jack hurries and opens a crypt at the bottom of the statue.
Jack exits down into the crypt as Zero hurries after him.

Zero barks.

INT. OOGIE BOOGIE'S DUNGEON - NIGHT

Santa Claus and Sally, tied to a table, look at Oogie Boogie.

                         SALLY
          You wait till Jack hears about this. By the time he's
          through with you, you'll be lucky if you . . .

                         MAYOR
                (pessimistic face) (over speaker)
          The king of Halloween . . .

Sally reacts with shock as she listens to the off-screen
Mayor.

EXT. HALLOWEEN LAND - NIGHT

Looking across the dark land to the treehouse. The Mayor
enters and drives his hearse.

                         MAYOR
                (pessimistic face) (over speaker)
          . . . has been blown to smithereens. Skeleton Jack is
          now a pile of dust.

INT. OOGIE BOOGIE'S DUNGEON - NIGHT

Santa Claus lies as Sally sits up and reacts with shock.

Sally gasps.

INT. HALLOWEEN TOWN CEMETERY - NIGHT

Jack enters through a crypt.

                         JACK
          Come on, Zero. Christmas isn't
          over yet.

Zero barks.

ASSISTANT EFFECTS ANIMATOR
Nathan Stanton recalled his experience working on Oogie Boogie's shadow animation. The completed animation could have easily been incorporated into the film as an optical film effect, but Director Henry Selick favored an approach more true to the traditions of stop-motion filmmaking. "They literally projected [the shadow] onto the set," Stanton recalled. Doing so meant the shadow animation would be shot one frame at a time, as if it were a puppet. Stanton was amazed. "It was mind-blowing that they would go that far to look authentic."

Jack hurries, camera dollying and tilting up with him to reveal the cemetery gate. Jack hurries through the gate. Jack runs, camera moving with him. Zero flies.

INT. OOGIE BOOGIE'S DUNGEON - NIGHT

Oogie Boogie walks toward Sally and Santa Claus, who are bound to the table.

              OOGIE BOOGIE
     What's that you were sayin' about luck,
     little rag doll?

EXT. HALLOWEEN LAND - NIGHT

Jack and Zero rush over a hill to reveal the treehouse.

EXT. TREEHOUSE - NIGHT

Jack and Zero enter from the ravine and hurry toward the base of the tree.

              SALLY (OFF)
     Help!

Jack stops as he hears Sally's voice. Camera dollies in to Jack, who listens to the sound of Sally's voice.

           SALLY (CONT'D) (OFF)
    Help! Helllllllp!

Zero whines.

Jack turns toward Zero and holds up a finger to quiet him.

                JACK
    Shh.

Camera cranes up into high angle as Jack climbs down a sapling into the ravine below the treehouse.

            OOGIE BOOGIE (OFF)
    Seven! It's Oogie's turn to boogie now.

Sally screams off camera.

INT. OOGIE BOOGIE'S DUNGEON - NIGHT

Oogie Boogie pushes on a lever that raises Santa Claus and Sally, lying on the table, toward a vat of stew, which is bubbling in the middle of the roulette wheel.

Sally screams.

> OOGIE BOOGIE
>
> One, two, three, four, five, six, seven. (laughs)

Sally and Santa Claus hang on to the table.

> SALLY
>
> Ohhh, hellllp!

EXT. TREEHOUSE - NIGHT

Jack leans and peers through a window into Oogie Boogie's dungeon.

> SANTA CLAUS (OFF)
>
> This can't be happening.

INT. OOGIE BOOGIE'S DUNGEON - NIGHT

Oogie Boogie dances around Sally and Santa Claus, who lie on the table.

> OOGIE BOOGIE (CONT'D)
>
> Ashes to ashes, and dust to dust.

Oogie Boogie gestures at Sally and Santa Claus with mock sympathy. Jack enters through the window, then slithers down the wall.

> OOGIE BOOGIE (CONT'D)
>
> Oh, I'm feeling weak . . .

Oogie Boogie leans menacingly toward Sally and Santa Claus.

> OOGIE BOOGIE (CONT'D)
>
> . . . with hunger. One more roll of the dice oughta do it. (laughs)

Oogie Boogie flings his dice out of frame. The dice hit against a skull , then drop down onto a table and both come up ones. Oogie Boogie enters, then he stops and peers down at the dice.

BLACK LITE   SEQ. 1200/31/32/33/34

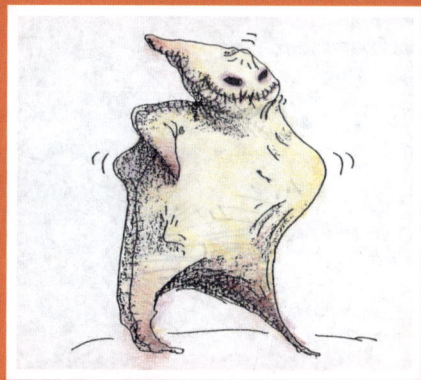

DELETED SCENE

Because stop-motion animation is so time intensive and costly, the general rule is "only shoot what you will use." Nearly all deleted scenes are done away with in the storyboard stage.

However, there is one extraordinary exception in *Nightmare*. It is a mostly completed scene, in color, that runs over two minutes. It begins by showing Lock, Shock, and Barrel listening to Oogie Boogie torment Sally and Santa through the pipe leading to their treehouse. The trio decides to take their elevator down to watch what's happening through a window into the dungeon, but first they grab movie snacks, popcorn, sodas, and candy. Once at the window, they giggle and laugh as Oogie Boogie berates his captives.

They then celebrate when they hear the Mayor's announcement that Jack has been reduced to a pile of dust. The scene ends when Jack climbs down the shaft, opens the elevator cage door, and the three miscreants scramble away. Visual Consultant Rick Heinrichs recalled that the scene was cut because it threw off the pacing of the action happening in Oogie Boogie's lair.

OOGIE BOOGIE (CONT'D)
What?! Snake eyes?!

Oogie Boogie slams his hand against the table. The dice roll over to a five and a six. Oogie Boogie smiles at the dice.

OOGIE BOOGIE (CONT'D)
Eleven! (laughs) Looks like I won the jackpot. Bye-bye, doll face and sandman.

Camera moves off Sally and Santa Claus to reveal the lever for the table. Oogie Boogie leans and works the lever, causing the table to tilt up toward the stew.

Sally wails off camera.

Santa Claus and Sally lie on the table as it tilts toward the stew.

Sally screams off camera.

Oogie Boogie stares down into the stew.

Sally screams off camera.

Oogie Boogie laughs.

Sally and Santa Claus do not enter from the table.

OOGIE BOOGIE (CONT'D)
What the . . . ?

Oogie Boogie reaches and grabs hold of the table. The table tilts to reveal Jack, who sits on the table. Oogie Boogie looks at Jack, sitting on the table, and reacts with shock.

Oogie Boogie gasps.

JACK
Hello, Oogie.

OOGIE BOOGIE
J-J-J-Jack. But they said you were dead. You must be . . .

Jack stands up and walks toward Oogie Boogie. Oogie Boogie (feet) presses down on a lever, which is in the floor.

                    OOGIE BOOGIE (CONT'D)
        . . . double dead!

The roulette wheel begins to turn. Jack maintains his balance.

                         JACK
        Uhh!

Playing cards rise up out of the roulette wheel. A king in a playing card swipes a sword at Jack, who avoids it.

Oogie Boogie laughs off camera.

Oogie Boogie walks on the roulette wheel as playing cards rise up
out of the roulette wheel. All the playing cards show pictures of kings, who hold their swords at the ready. Jack ducks beneath the swords as they swing at him. Oogie Boogie, standing on the roulette wheel as it turns, looks at Jack.

                      OOGIE BOOGIE
        Well, come on, bone man!

Camera looks through a barred window to Zero, who is too large to squeeze through.

Zero barks.

Sally and Santa Claus, hiding behind a suit of armor, look at Jack. Jack tumbles across the roulette wheel, camera moving with him as he avoids the flailing swords. Oogie Boogie gestures at off-screen Jack with frustration.

                    OOGIE BOOGIE (CONT'D)
                        (chuckling)
        Oooo! Ha!

The playing cards close up their swords and begin to exit down into the roulette wheel. Jack enters and walks as the slot machine gunslingers enter and move toward him. Oogie Boogie, standing on the roulette wheel as it spins, gestures at the slot machine gunslingers.

OOGIE BOOGIE (CONT'D)

    Fire!

The slot machine gunslingers aim their pistols at Jack. Camera moves past the slot machine gunslingers to Jack, who leaps up onto their pistols. They fire their pistols past Jack. Oogie Boogie is carried on the spinning roulette wheel, then he looks at the slot matchine gunslingers with shock.

OOGIE BOOGIE (CONT'D)

    Oh!

Oogie Boogie turns and starts to run. Oogie Boogie tries to run, but the spinning roulette wheel carries him toward the gunfire of the slot machine gunslingers.

Oogie Boogie grunts.

Oogie Boogie makes a desperate lunge. Oogie Boogie lands on the floor and pushes a button. A whirling sawmill blade descends toward Jack. Santa Claus and Sally look nervously at Jack.

SALLY

    Jack, look out!

Jack stands atop the pistols of the slot machine gunslingers as the sawmill blade descends toward him. Jack turns and looks at the sawmill blade. Jack leaps and exits as the sawmill blade moves and slices off the pistols in the hands of the slot machine gunslingers. Oogie Boogie stands on the roulette wheel as it moves. Jack enters and lands on the roulette wheel.

Oogie Boogie gasps.

Oogie Boogie steps, then a panel rises up and launches him through the air. Oogie Boogie flies through the air and grabs onto the eightball, which is attached to the ceiling by a rod. Oogie Boogie smirks at Jack.

OOGIE BOOGIE

    So long, Jack!

The eightball retracts up toward the ceiling, camera tilting
up with it. Jack glares up at Oogie Boogie. A string from Oogie
Boogie's sack hangs down into frame.

Oogie Boogie laughs.

                         JACK
           How dare you treat my friends so shamefully.

Jack pulls down on the string. Oogie Boogie is carried up
into the air on the eightball, camera tilting up with him. The
string pulls out of Oogie Boogie's sack, causing bugs, spiders,
and creepie-crawlies to fall out.

                     OOGIE BOOGIE
           Huh? No, no . . .

Camera tilts up, off Jack, to reveal Oogie Boogie's face as his
sack falls completely off.

                 OOGIE BOOGIE (CONT'D)
                      (in falsetto)
           . . . no, no! No, no, Jack! No!

Oogie Boogie's form, composed of bugs, snakes, and creepie-
crawlies, is completely exposed.

        (The bugs' overlapping, indistinct squealing and murmuring
             continues under following scenes and dialogue)

                 OOGIE BOOGIE (CONT'D)
           Now look what you've done!

Oogie Boogie stands on the eightball as bugs fall off his body.

                 OOGIE BOOGIE (CONT'D)
                      (wailing)
           My bugs. My bugs. My bugs.

Oogie Boogie's body begins to completely dissipate. Bugs fall
off Oogie Boogie and land in the boiling stew.

                    OOGIE BOOGIE (CONT'D)
                         (wailing)
        My bugs. My bugs. My bugs.

Sally stares at the stew with shock. Jack stares grimly at
the stew.

                 OOGIE BOOGIE (CONT'D) (OFF)
        My bugs. My bugs. My bugs.

Zero floats down through the air, camera tilting with him. A
single green bug scurries across the floor, camera dollying
with him.

                        GREEN BUG
        My bugs. My bugs.

Santa Claus's foot enters and crushes the green bug beneath
it. Santa looks angrily at Jack. Jack looks regretfully at
Santa Claus.

                          JACK
        Forgive me, Mister Claws. I'm afraid I've made a terrible
        mess of your holiday.

Jack pulls Santa Claus's hat out of his jacket and holds it
out toward Santa Claus.

                        SANTA CLAUS
        Bumpy sleigh ride, Jack?

Santa Claus grabs his hat out of Jack's hands. Santa Claus
gestures at Jack with exasperation.

                     SANTA CLAUS (CONT'D)
        The next time you get the urge to take over someone
        else's holiday, I'd listen to her.

Santa Claus points at Sally. Sally smiles at Santa Claus.

                     SANTA CLAUS (CONT'D)
        She's the only one who makes any sense around this
        insane asylum.

Santa Claus puts his hat on his head. Camera looks past
Santa Claus to Jack, who looks sheepishly at him. Sally
stands behind the suit of armor. Santa Claus walks.

SANTA CLAUS (CONT'D)
Skeletons and boogie men and . . .

JACK
I hope there's still time.

Santa Claus stops, then he turns and
looks at Jack.

SANTA CLAUS
To fix Christmas? Of course, there is! I'm Santa Claus!

Santa Claus puts his finger to the side of his nose. Santa
Claus flies up into the air, camera tilting up with him to
reveal the pipe. Santa Claus exits through the pipe. Jack
stares up at the pipe as Sally walks up behind Jack.

SALLY
He'll fix things, Jack. He knows what to do.

Jack looks down sadly, then he turns toward Sally. Camera
looks past Sally to Jack, who looks quizzically at her.

JACK
How did you get down here, Sally?

Sally twists her hands nervously.

SALLY
Oh, I, I was trying to . . .

Camera looks past Jack to Sally, who looks hesitatingly at
him.

SALLY (CONT'D)
Well, I wanted to . . . to . . .

Past Sally to Jack, who looks thoughtfully at her. Jack
gestures toward himself.

                         JACK
        To help me.

Sally turns and looks down shyly.

                        SALLY
        I couldn't let you just—

Jack lays his hand on Sally's shoulder.

                         JACK
        Sally. I can't believe . . .

Sally starts to turn toward Jack. Past Jack to Sally, who looks
hopefully at him.

                    JACK (CONT'D)
        . . . I never realized that you—

A bright shaft of light illuminates them. Camera moves back as
Sally and Jack look up at the off-screen Mayor.

                        MAYOR
                  (optimistic face)
        Jack! Jack!

Zero looks up at the Mayor. Lock, Shock, Barrel, and the Mayor,
whose optimistic face is turned forward, stand in the pipe
opening and look down at Jack.

                        BARREL
        Here he is!

                         LOCK
        Alive!

                        SHOCK
        Just like we said!

The Mayor drops a rope ladder down toward Jack.

                        MAYOR
                  (optimistic face)
        Grab a hold, my boy!

Jack and Sally step to the rope ladder. Jack grabs hold of the rope ladder, then he takes Sally's hand with his other hand. Jack and Sally are jerked up out of frame on the rope ladder.

                    JACK & SALLY
     Whoa!

INT. RADIO STATION - NIGHT

The female radio announcer reads from a sheet of copy.

                    FEMALE RADIO ANNOUNCER
                  (reading into microphone)
     Good news, folks. Santa Claus, the one and only . . .

INT. HOWIE'S HOUSE - NIGHT

Howie is trapped as the Jack-in-the-box jumps up and down. Santa Claus enters and grabs the Jack-in-the-box, then he jerks the Jack-in-the-box out of frame.

                    FEMALE RADIO ANNOUNCER
                      (over speaker)
     . . . has finally been spotted. Old Saint Nick appears
     to be traveling . . .

Santa Claus reenters and holds out a candy cane toward Howie.

INT. WANDA'S HOUSE/HALLWAY - NIGHT

The Evil Toy Duck and the doll bang against the door of the children's bedroom.

                    FEMALE RADIO ANNOUNCER
                   (reading over speaker)
     . . . at supersonic speed.

The Evil Toy Duck quacks. Santa Claus enters, then he jerks the doll and the Evil Toy Duck out of frame. Santa Claus reenters, then he puts a teddy bear and a sailboat down on the floor.

                    FEMALE RADIO ANNOUNCER (CONT'D)
                         (reading over speaker)
           He's setting things right, bringing joy and cheer . . .

The door opens to reveal Wanda and Ronnie, who look down at
the toys and smile.

INT. TIMMIE'S HOUSE - NIGHT

Timmie holds the shrunken head. Santa Claus enters and grabs
the shrunken head, then he exits with it.

                       FEMALE RADIO ANNOUNCER
                         (reading over speaker)
            . . . wherever he goes. Yes, folks, Kris Kringle has
            pulled it out of the bag . . .

Santa Claus reenters and hands a puppy dog to Timmie.

EXT. HALLOWEEN TOWN SQUARE- NIGHT

The cauldron shows an image of the female radio announcer.

                       FEMALE RADIO ANNOUNCER
                        (reading into microphone)
            . . . and delivered Christmas to excited children . . .

Camera dollies off the cauldron to reveal the Witches, who
sleep on the ground. All the witches are wearing sleeping
masks.

                    FEMALE RADIO ANNOUNCER (CONT'D)
            . . . all over the world.

Camera holds as the Witches wake up and pull of their
sleeping masks. The gate opens and the Mayor drives the hearse
through the gateway. Jack, Lock, Shock, and Barrel sit on top
the hearse and Sally sits in the passenger seat.

OOGIE BOOGIE MAN

Oogie Boogie was not part of the original "The Nightmare Before Christmas" poem. He was created by Tim Burton later, to be the antagonist for the film. While Oogie Boogie may have originated as the standard bad-guy stereotype, it wasn't until Danny Elfman wrote the character's song "Oogie Boogie's Song" that his personality was defined.

Stage and film actor Ken Page provided Oogie Boogie's voice. Burton and Elfman thought his rich baritone was perfect for the role, and they had a similar musical style in mind for the character. As it turned out, they both had happy memories of the great jazz singer Cab Calloway and his rendition of the classic song "Minnie the Moocher"—Burton from an old Max Fleischer cartoon, and Elfman from his early days with his band, The Mystic Knights of the Oingo Boingo, when one of their first performances paid homage to Calloway. That style was what they wanted for Oogie Boogie, and Page delivered it perfectly.

But Oogie Boogie's tough-guy reputation doesn't come just from his song. The two-foot-tall Oogie Boogie puppet was quite a challenge to manipulate. As animator Mike Belzer recalled, "I had to dig in with my foot and physically push [him]," he said. "He's so huge and there's so much foam, and the armature needs to be very tight. [I was] literally wrestling with the puppet!"

FINALE

La, la, la
La, la, la, la
La, la, la
La, la, la, la

Jack!
Jack's back!
Jack?
Jack's okay.
He's all right.
It's Jack!

Jack's okay and he's back okay
He's all right
Let's shout. Make a fuss
Scream it out!
Wheeee!

Jack is back now, everyone sing
In the town of Halloween

It's great to be home!

· DEAD CAT ·

Happy Halloween!

Merry Christmas!

What's this?
What's this?
I haven't got a clue

What's this?
Why it's completely new

What's this?
Must be a Christmas thing

What's this?
It's really very strange

This is Halloween, Halloween, Halloween
What's this? What's this?
What's this? What's this?

Careful, my precious jewel

My dearest friend, if you don't mind
I'd like to join you by your side
Where we can gaze into the stars

And sit together, now and forever
For it is plain as anyone can see
We're simply meant to be

EXT. HALLOWEEN TOWN/CEMETERY - NIGHT

Jack and Sally lower their hands and step toward one
another. Jack and Sally, standing atop the Spiral Hill,
kiss. Camera dollies back slowly to reveal Zero, who flies
and looks at Sally and Jack. Zero then flies up into the
sky, camera tilting up with him, off Jack and Sally. Zero
flies and exits into the dark night sky. A Christmas star
appears in the sky and twinkles brightly. The scene fades
to black.

        THE END

CAST

JACK SKELLINGTON (SINGING)/BARREL

Danny Elfman

JACK SKELLINGTON (SPEAKING)

Chris Sarandon

MAYOR

Glenn Shadix

DR. FINKELSTEIN

William Hickey

LOCK

Paul Reubens

SALLY/SHOCK

Catherine O'Hara

OOGIE BOOGIE

Ken Page

SANTA CLAUS

Edward Ivory

ILLUSTRATOR AND PHOTO CREDITS

All illustrations and pictures created by Disney Studio Artists and Photographers, excluding:

iv, Jack and Santa, Tim Burton
5, Jack's house, Deane Taylor/Kendal Cronkhite
6, Monster (bottom left), Jack and Zero (bottom right), Tim Burton
6, Timmie's bedroom, Kendal Cronkhite
7, 136, Sally, Tim Burton
7, 20, Jack and Santa, Tim Burton
8, Stack of gift boxes, Richard Improta and Tim Wollweber
13, Forest with tree doors, Tim Burton
14, Halloween Town, Tim Burton
18, Scarecrow Pumpkin King, Kendal Cronkhite
19, Jack's house/pumpkin patch, Deane Taylor
27, All images, Tim Burton
29, Jack's lament, Tim Burton
32, Sally, Kendal Cronkhite
36, Halloween Town set, Elizabeth J. Annas
37, Suburbia cemetery set, Elizabeth J. Annas
38, Forest, Kendal Cronkhite
38, Halloween Town, Kelly Asbury
39, Jack's stairway, Kendal Cronkhite
46, Christmas Town, Kendal Cronkhite
47, Christmas Town train, Kendal Cronkhite
49, Christmas Town, Kendal Cronkhite
50, Tim Burton and Henry Selick, Elizabeth J. Annas
50, Henry Selick, Elizabeth J. Annas
50, Tim Burton, Elizabeth J. Annas
53, Illustration, Tim Burton
53, SF Studios, Elizabeth J. Annas
54, Illustrator, Elizabeth J. Annas
62, Hearse, Kelly Asbury and Deane Taylor
66, Christmas Tree, Tim Burton
69, Christmas Town gingerbread house, Kendal Cronkhite
75, Jack's house, Kelly Asbury
76, Dr. Finkelstein's laboratory (bottom right), Kelly Asbury

78, Sally, Tim Burton
79, Sally, Tim Burton
82, Jack in electric chair pencil, Kelly Asbury
82, Jack in electric chair color, Kelly Asbury
85, Jack (bottom left), Tim Burton
97, Lock, Shock, and Barrel, Kelly Asbury
110, Jack, deleted scene, Miguel Domingo Cachuela
111, Oogie Boogie, deleted scene 1, Miguel Domingo Cachuela
111, Oogie Boogie, deleted scene 2, Miguel Domingo Cachuela
111, Sally, deleted scene, Miguel Domingo Cachuela
111, Dr. Finkelstein, deleted scene 1, Miguel Domingo Cachuela
111, Dr. Finkelstein, deleted scene 2, Miguel Domingo Cachuela
112, Tree doors in forest, Tim Burton
120, Zero, Tim Burton
124, Mrs. Claus, Kendal Cronkhite
124, Santa opening door, Tim Burton
131, Filming stop motion animation (top), Elizabeth J. Annas
131, Filming stop motion animation (bottom left), Elizabeth J. Annas
131, Filming stop motion animation (bottom right), Elizabeth J. Annas
132, Jack, Tim Burton
136, All images, Tim Burton
139, Oogie Boogie in lair, Kelly Asbury
142, All images, Elizabeth J. Annas
145, Sally (upper right), Tim Burton
148, Jack and Zero, Tim Burton
151, Sally, deleted scene, Miguel Domingo Cachuela
153, Sally (upper right), Tim Burton
153, Sally (bottom left), Tim Burton
153, Sally (bottom right), Kendal Cronkhite
155, Jack and Timmie, Tim Burton
161, All images, Elizabeth J. Annas

MUSIC CREDITS

"This is Halloween"
Words and Music by Danny Elfman
© 1993 Buena Vista Music Company (BMI)
All Rights Reserved. Used with Permission

"Jack's Lament"
Words and Music by Danny Elfman
© 1993 Buena Vista Music Company (BMI)
All Rights Reserved. Used with Permission

"What's This?"
Words and Music by Danny Elfman
© 1993 Buena Vista Music Company (BMI)
All Rights Reserved. Used with Permission

"Town Meeting Song"
Words and Music by Danny Elfman
© 1993 Buena Vista Music Company (BMI)
All Rights Reserved. Used with Permission

"Jack's Obsession"
Words and Music by Danny Elfman
© 1993 Buena Vista Music Company (BMI)
All Rights Reserved. Used with Permission

"Kidnap the Sandy Claws"
Words and Music by Danny Elfman
© 1993 Buena Vista Music Company (BMI)
All Rights Reserved. Used with Permission

"Making Christmas"
Words and Music by Danny Elfman
© 1993 Buena Vista Music Company (BMI)
All Rights Reserved. Used with Permission

"Oogie Boogie's Song"
Words and Music by Danny Elfman
© 1993 Buena Vista Music Company (BMI)
All Rights Reserved. Used with Permission

"Sally's Song"
Words and Music by Danny Elfman
© 1993 Buena Vista Music Company (BMI)
All Rights Reserved. Used with Permission

"Poor Jack"
Words and Music by Danny Elfman
© 1993 Buena Vista Music Company (BMI)
All Rights Reserved. Used with Permission

"Finale/Reprise"
Words and Music by Danny Elfman
© 1993 Buena Vista Music Company (BMI)
All Rights Reserved. Used with Permissio

Every effort has been made to credit the illustrators
and photographers and to obtain the necessary
permissions. In the instance of a missing attribution,
the publisher would be pleased to insert the appropriate
acknowledgment in subsequent editions.

Please direct any inquiries to Studio Press, an imprint
of Bonnier Books UK, 4th Floor, Victoria House,
Bloomsbury Square, London WC1B 4DA

ACKNOWLEDGMENTS

Deepest gratitude to Tim Burton and Rick Heinrichs for
their wonderful collaboration and support of this book.
Their behind-the-scenes stories and memories from working
on the film have added a unique and artistic perspective.

Huge thank-you to Fox Carney, Doug Engalla, and Jackie Vasquez
at the Walt Disney Animation Research Library for their invaluable
help with the artwork seen in this book. Their exhaustive research
and expert knowledge in Disney art and history made it possible
for these stories to come to life.

Many thanks to Chelsea Alon
for her continued guidance and support.